FOUR PLAY

BY JAKE BRUNGER

Four Play was commissioned by Old Vic New Voices
as part of the TS Eliot Commissions.

It was developed by Fools & Kings, D.E.M. Productions
and Theatre503 and received its world premiere
on 16 February 2016 at Theatre503, London.

FOUR PLAY
BY JAKE BRUNGER

CAST

Rafe	Cai Brigden
Pete	Michael Gilbert
Michael	Peter Hannah
Andrew	Michael James

CREATIVE TEAM

Director	Jonathan O'Boyle
Designer	Cecilia Carey
Lighting Designer	Jack Weir
Sound Designer	Max Perryment
Assistant Director	Hannah Hauer-King
Design Assistant	Isobel Pellow

PRODUCTION TEAM

Producers	Jessica Campbell, Jack Sain & Ramin Sabi
Associate Producer	Ceri Lothian
Production Manager	James Ashby
Stage Manager	Rike Berg
Press Representation	Chloe Nelkin Consulting

CAST

CAI BRIGDEN (Rafe)
Cai trained at Guildhall School of Music and Drama. His theatre credits include *Another Country* (Trafalgar Studios/Chichester Festival Theatre); *Super John* (Firehouse Creative Productions) and *Butley* (Nimax Theatres). Television and film credits include *Chewing Gum* (Retort Comedy, Channel 4); *Doctors*, *Casualty* (BBC) and *The Telemachy* (Matchbox Productions).

MICHAEL GILBERT (Pete)
Michael recently graduated from the Oxford School of Drama. His theatre credits include *Treasure* (Finborough) and his credits at Oxford include *Lines in the Sand*, *All Day Permanent Red*, *All My Sons*, *A Midsummer Night's Dream*, *The Country Wife* and *The Idiot*.

PETER HANNAH (Michael)
Peter trained at RADA. His theatre credits include *Shakespeare in Love* (Noël Coward); *Lysistrata* [rehearsed reading] (Almeida); *The Pooki* [workshop] (Park Theatre); *One Arm* (Southwark Playhouse); *Mock Tudor* (Pleasance Courtyard); *A Clockwork Orange* (Nottingham Playhouse); *Paradise Lost* [workshop] (Birmingham Rep); *The Wallace* [reading] (Finborough). Film and television credits include *Mr Turner* (Thin Man Films) and *Doctor Who* (BBC).

MICHAEL JAMES (Andrew)
Michael recently graduated from Mountview Academy of Theatre Arts where he was the recipient of the 2015 Gyearbuor Asante Prize for Acting. His theatre credits include *Someone Else's Shoes* (Little Fly Theatre) and *The Last Days of Troy* (Shakespeare's Globe). His television credits include *Doctors* (BBC). His credits at Mountview include *Karagula* – a new play by Philip Ridley, *Her Naked Skin*, *As You Like It* and *Summerfolk*.

CREATIVES

JAKE BRUNGER (Writer)

Jake grew up in Nottingham and now lives in London. He read Drama at Bristol University.

As a musical-theatre writer, with his collaborator composer Pippa Cleary, his credits (as book writer and lyricist) include *Treasure Island* (Singapore Repertory Theatre); *Prodigy* (National Youth Music Theatre/St James); *The Secret Diary of Adrian Mole Aged 13 ¾* (Leicester Curve); *Red Riding Hood* (Singapore Repertory Theatre/Pleasance); *The Great British Soap Opera* (Edinburgh/Jermyn Street); and *Jet Set Go!* (Edinburgh/Theatre503/Jermyn Street). He co-wrote the lyrics for *The Snow Gorilla* at the Rose Theatre, Kingston.

As a playwright, Jake's credits include *Brave New Worlds* (Nabokov/Soho); *People Like Us* (Pleasance/TS Eliot US/UK Exchange: Vineyard, New York); *Chavs* (Lyric Hammersmith Studio); *'AVE IT* (Old Vic Tunnels); *Pub Quiz* (Manchester Royal Exchange Studio, which he also directed) and *Sam's Game* (Lakeside Arts Centre, dir. Indhu Rubasingham).

JONATHAN O'BOYLE (Director)

Jonathan is an Associate Director at Theatre503. He trained at the Central School of Speech and Drama and Birkbeck, University of London, and is currently Trainee Associate Director at Chichester Festival Theatre.

Directing credits include *Broken Glass* (Central School of Speech and Drama); *Sense of an Ending* (Theatre503, Time Out Critics' Choice); *The Surplus* (Young Vic); *The Verb, To Love, Made In Britain* (Old Red Lion); *All The Ways to Say Goodbye* (Young Vic, 5 Plays); *Bash Latterday Plays* (Trafalgar Studios/Old Red Lion, Time Out Critics' Choice); *Water Under the Board* (Theatre503); *Last Online Today, Guinea Pigs* (Crucible New Writers' Project, Sheffield Crucible Studio); *Credit* and *The Monster Bride* (Tristan Bates).

Associate Director credits include *The Judas Kiss* (Chichester Festival Theatre/Toronto/New York); *Mack and Mabel* (Chichester Festival Theatre/UK tour); *Bull* (Young Vic/Sheffield Crucible/New York); *This Is My Family* (Sheffield Theatres/UK tour); *Amadeus* (Chichester Festival Theatre); *The Scottsboro Boys* (Young Vic); *Manon* (Royal Opera House); *My Fair Lady, The Village Bike* (Sheffield Crucible); *Someone Who'll Watch Over Me* (Southwark Playhouse).

CECILIA CAREY (Designer)

Cecilia is a set and costume designer for theatre and site-specific works. She trained on the Motley Theatre Design course. Recent credits include *The National Youth Theatre Rep Shows 2015* (Ambassadors; dir. Emily Lim, dir. Pia Furtado, dir. Anna Niland); *The Late Henry Moss* (Southwark Playhouse; nominated for Off West End Best Set Designer; dir. Mel Hillyard); *The Brolly Project* (Young Vic; dir. Mimi Poskitt); *The Surplus* (Young Vic; dir. Jonathan O'Boyle); *About Her* (London Film Festival 2016); *Sense of an Ending* (Theatre503; dir. Jonathan O'Boyle); *The Interventionists* (Lyric Hammersmith; dir Bad Physics); *Pioneer* (Curious Directive, Fringe First Award); *The Great Train Dance* (Severn Valley Railway; dir. Rosie Kay); *The Red Helicopter* (Almeida; dir Tessa Walker).

Associate Designer credits include *Disco Pigs* (touring) and *OMG!* (The Place/Sadler's Wells). Cecilia assisted Es Devlin on the 'Take That' Tour, 'Kanye West Gold' Tour, and the Closing Ceremony of the London 2012 Olympics.

JACK WEIR (Lighting Designer)

Jack trained at the Guildhall School and is recipient of the 2014 ETC Award for Lighting Design. Credits include *No Villain* (Old Red Lion); *Stitching* (The White Bear); *My Children! My Africa!* (Trafalgar Studios); *African Gothic, Muswell Hill* (Park Theatre); *Bruises, Misalliance* (Tabard); *Fear & Misery, Roadshow, The Spitfire Grill* (Union); *The Sum of Us, Rise Like a Phoenix, Bathhouse, The Boys Upstairs* (Above The Stag); *All-Male Pirates of Penzance* (UK tour); *Princess Ida, Three Guys Singing, Armstrong's War* (Finborough); *Wild Worlds* (VAULT Festival); *Grim – The Musical* (Charing Cross); *Hamlet* (Riverside Studios), *Richard III* (Upstairs at The Gatehouse); *Passing By* (Tristan Bates) and *Titus Andronicus* (Arcola).

MAX PERRYMENT (Sound Designer)

Max Perryment is a composer and sound designer. He has composed extensively for commiericials and television adverts. His most recent work for theatre includes *Creditors, The Remarkable Case of K., The Surplus* (Young Vic); *Sense of an Ending,* (Theatre503); *And Then Come The Nightjars* (Theatre503/Bristol Old Vic); *Three Lions* (St James/tour) and *Black Dog Gold Fish* (VAULT Festival). He was recently nominated for an Offie and a Broadway World Award for Best Sound Design.

HANNAH HAUER-KING (Assistant Director)

Hannah Hauer-King is a freelance theatre director and co-founder of Damsel Productions. She was Resident Assistant Director at Soho Theatre, and recent credits include *Dry Land* (Jermyn Street); associate on *Titus Andronicus* (Smooth Faced Gentlemen, Edinburgh Fringe/Greenwich); *PLAY* (Old Red Lion); *Pool (No Water), Spring Awakening* (M&B Theatre, Washington DC); *Don't Frighten Her* (Georgetown University). Assistant directing credits include *I Kiss Your Heart* and *Symphony* (Soho); *Daytona* (Theatre Royal Haymarket) and *Radiant Vermin* (Soho). Upcoming productions include *Brute* (Soho); *CLAY* (Pleasance, London) and associate director to Daniel Kramer on *Tristan and Isolde* (ENO).

ISOBEL PELLOW (Design Assistant)

Isobel studied at Warwick University during which time she worked at the Loft Theatre in Leamington Spa. Since graduating, she has worked on costume design for the Ashcroft Theatre, Old Red Lion, English Touring Opera, The Place and as costume designer at the Oxford Playhouse and the Old Fire Station, Oxford. She was the design assistant on D.E.M's production of *Clickbait* (Theatre503).

JAMES ASHBY (Production Manager)

James trained at East 15 Acting School, studying carpentry as his major. He now works for The Scenery Shop as Production Carpenter, where his credits include *4000 Days* (Park Theatre) and *The Den* (The Hive, Hackney). Production Management credits include *Clickbait* (Theatre503); *Treasure* (Finborough); *Sense of an Ending* (Theatre503); *Donkey Heart* (Trafalgar Studios); *The Njogel Opera* (Tête à tête Opera Festival) and Assistant Production Manager on *The Little Green Swallow* (Peacock).

RIKE BERG (Stage Manager)

Rike graduated from the Bauhaus University Weimar in Germany, and has worked on various theatre productions in Sweden and the UK. Her most recent credits as Stage Manager/Assistant Stage Manager include *The Woman in Black* (Gothenburg English Studio Theatre/Sweden tour); *Belongings* (GEST); *Upper Cut* (Southwark Playhouse); *Sense of an Ending* (Theatre503); *Lines* (The Yard) and *Clickbait* (Theatre503). Since moving to London, Rike has also worked for the Pleasance London, the Gate Theatre, the Bush Theatre and the Royal Albert Hall.

DEUS EX MACHINA PRODUCTIONS (Producer)

DEM Productions was set up by producers Jessica Campbell and Ramin Sabi to produce high-quality plays in London's Off West End. DEM has been nominated for the 2016 OffWestEnd Award for Best Producer. Jess and Ramin have produced seven productions, which have accrued nine OffWestEnd Awards, six Broadway World Award nominations, and over fifty four- or five-star reviews between them.

Productions include *How I Learned to Drive* and *A Bright Room Called Day* (Southwark Playhouse); *Sense of an Ending*, *A First World Problem* (Theatre503); *Stink Foot* (The Yard); *Donkey Heart* (Trafalgar Studios) and *Piranha Heights* (Old Red Lion).

Jessica is the Producer and Head of Marketing at Theatre503 where she has produced *And Then Come The Nightjars* (also at Bristol Old Vic) and *Valhalla*. She has worked for James Seabright Productions and Old Vic New Voices.

Ramin recently co-produced *Gypsy* starring Imelda Staunton (Savoy, West End). Other producing credits include *Let It Be* (Garrick) and *Annie* (UK and Ireland tour). He is also producer and CFO for Zoya Films where he has produced a number of commercials, short films and music videos. He is currently executive producer on independent feature film *Butterfly Kisses*.

FOOLS & KINGS (Producer)

Fools and Kings was established by Jack Sain and Jessica Campbell. Jack Sain trained at LAMDA and his credits as a director include *Four Play* (Old Vic New Voices); *How I Learned to Drive* (Southwark Playhouse); *That's the Spirit!* (RWR/Theatre503); *Angels in America* (Oxford Playhouse); *Machinal* (Oxford Castle/C Venues/Arcola) and *Cymbeline* (Tabard). His credits as a producer include *Robbie Wakes* and *Mr Kolpert* (Edinburgh Fringe); *Oleanna* (Tristan Bates) and *A First World Problem* (Theatre503). He is the Resident Assistant Director at the Donmar Warehouse, where his upcoming assisting includes *Welcome Home, Captain Fox!* (dir. Blanche McIntyre), *Elegy* (dir. Josie Rourke) and *Faith Healer* (dir. Lyndsey Turner). He also works as a photographer.

CERI LOTHIAN (Associate Producer)

Ceri graduated from the University of Kent with a first-class honours degree in Drama and English Literature in July 2015. She worked as Resident Assistant Producer at Theatre503 from May – November 2015, and was on the producing team for the inaugural Theatre503 Award Season plays *And Then Come The Nightjars* and *Valhalla*. Other producing credits whilst studying include *Cabaret* (Gulbenkian Theatre); *Bad* (Colyer-Fergusson Music Hall) and *Spring Awakening* (Marlowe Theatre Studio).

Thanks

Kirsten Adam
David Adkin
David Benedictus
Sue Emmas
Alexander Ferris
Nick Frankfort
Annie, Jon, Richard and all at the Jerwood Space
Sara and Robbie Lowenstein
Paul Robinson
Abubakar Salim
David Shields
Bertie Taylor-Smith
Catherine Kodicek at the Young Vic
Tom Wright
Dugie Young

Thanks from the author

Jack Sain, Kirsty Patrick Ward, Harriet Pennington Legh, Steve
Winter, Alexander Ferris, and the Old Vic New Voices Festival reading
cast for their invaluable development of the play: Jeremy Irvine,
Richard Madden, Joshua McCord and Tom Rhys Harries.

This production is generously supported by

The Martin Bowley Charitable Trust
Chris Smith
Peter Gill

SUBSIDISED REHEARSAL FACILITIES PROVIDED BY

JERWOOD SPACE

Theatre503 is the award-winning home of groundbreaking plays.

Led by Artistic Director Paul Robinson, Theatre503 is a flagship fringe venue committed to producing new work that is game-changing, relevant, surprising, mischievous, visually thrilling and theatrical. We are the smallest theatre to win an Olivier Award and we offer more opportunities to new writers than anywhere in the UK.

We couldn't do what we do without our volunteers:
Andrei Vornicu, Annabel Pemberton, Bethany Doherty, Charlotte Mulliner, Chidi Chukwu, Damian Robertson, Danielle Wilson, Fabienne Gould, George Linfield, James Hansen, Joanna Lallay, Kelly Agredo, Ken Hawes, Larner Taylor, Mandy Nicholls, Mark Doherty, Mike Murgaz, Nicole Marie, Rahim Dhanji, Rosie Akerman, Tess Hardy.

Theatre503 is supported by:
Philip and Chris Carne, Cas Donald, Gregory Dunlop, Angela Hyde-Courtney and the Audience Club, Stephanie Knauf, Sumintra Latchman, Katherine Malcom, Georgia Oetker, Francesca Ortona, Geraldine Sharpe-Newton.

Support Theatre503
Help us take risks on new writers and produce the plays other theatres can't, or won't. Together we can discover the writers of tomorrow and make some of the most exciting theatre in the country. With memberships ranging from £23 to £1003 there is a chance to get involved no matter what your budget, to help us remain '**arguably the most important theatre in Britain today**' (*Guardian*).

Benefits range from priority notice of our work and news, access to sold out shows, ticket deals, and opportunities to attend parties and peek into rehearsals. Visit t**heatre503.com** or call **020 7978 7040** for more details.

Theatre503, 503 Battersea Park Rd, London SW11 3BW
020 7978 7040 | www.theatre503.com
@Theatre503 | Facebook.com/theatre503

FOUR PLAY

Jake Brunger

Characters

RAFE, *mid-twenties*
PETE, *mid-twenties*
MICHAEL, *late twenties*
ANDREW, *mid-twenties*

This text went to press before the end of rehearsals and so may differ slightly from the play as performed.

A Note on the Text

This is a pretty open text.
I didn't want to use the words [*pause*] or [*beat*] which I
usually use.
So instead I've made up a thing like this: [–]
It means a beat, or a pause, or a breath, or a change.
It's up to you.
But just observe that it's there... don't run over it.
[–]
On the whole, this play is meant to be performed quite quickly.
Words are on different lines but
it
shouldn't
slow
things
down
If anything it should speed it up.
Get to the next line quickly sort of thing.
[–]
Oh.
One more thing.
I also use (brackets) which are asides, or afterthoughts.
But [*square brackets*] are not meant to be said out loud; they're
just to clarify the meaning.
(does that make... [*sense*]...?)
Good.
That's everything you need to know.

One

RAFE, PETE *and* MICHAEL.

RAFE So the thing is.
Okay.
What the thing is.
Is that.
We've been together a long time.
Right?
Like, seven years?
(well, seven-and-a-half if we're actually being specific…)
We met at university.
(End of our first year.)
And we sort of got together in secret at first.
(Neither of us were actually out at the time.)
But our relationship blossomed and now…
Here we are.
Seven years later.
(Well, seven-and-a-half if we're being… specific…)
And we have good jobs…
Yes.
Quite a nice flat.
(rented, sure, but… one thing at a time…)
And Pete's earning money now.
(I am as well…)
(not quite as much but…)
We're doing alright.
Is what I'm trying to say.
[–]
But the thing is.
You see.
What the thing is.

Is that.

[–]

Pete is.

(And I…)

We are the only… person.

(man/boy (whatever)

That the other one has… *been* with.

[–]

And

(As I'm sure you know…)

That's unusual in our world.

I mean, in *any* world that's unusual; to be so

blissfully happy in such a long-term relationship.

But particularly in *our* world, you know.

It's strange.

[–]

So what it is…

Michael.

We have a sort of conundrum:

We love each other. (Very much.)

And we have… good sex.

(We think)

But it's the only sex we've ever had.

I mean, we've never even kissed another guy.

Never even brushed

(Well maybe brushed…)

against someone.

Like, even in a club.

Cos we don't go to clubs.

Why would we?

Clubs are a place where single people go to pull

other single people who are usually drunk.

[–]

I mean we've talked about our options:

– A break. (we don't want that)

– An escort. (no way)

(we don't agree with that…)

(…paying someone for their body? We really sort

of frown on that)

– Picking up a guy in a club (we don't know what that could lead to)

(disease-wise, right?)

– Or finding someone online…

It's always a risk.

(I mean you saw that documentary about Russia, right?)

(no one wants to get knived, do they?)

(is it knived or knifed…?)

(Knifed, yes.)

[–]

So instead we arrived at something slightly…

Different.

We went through our mutual friends on Facebook.

People that we like.

And we came across…

You.

We clicked on.

You.

[–]

Because what we're looking for is someone who…

We're not *particularly* close to.

(Not like, enemies or anything.)

But someone that… neither of us knows better.

Someone we both like *physically* obviously…

– Facially.

– Personality.

But who isn't going to cause problems.

Bump into us in Sainsbury's or…

Give us HIV.

Pete and I arrived on you as the solution to our problem.

Someone we can…

'Enjoy the company of.'

But one time only.

Literally only once.

Simply to solve our 'conundrum'.

[–]

So…
What do you think?
[–]
What
Do
You
Think?

MICHAEL   [–]
I.
[–]
Well…
[–]

RAFE   You can…
Take your time.

MICHAEL   [–]
I have.
[–]
A boyfriend.

RAFE   Yes.

MICHAEL   Andrew.

RAFE   Right.

MICHAEL   And.

RAFE   We know that.
Obviously.
(we probably should have said)
That's why we chose you.

MICHAEL   For Andrew?

RAFE   Yes.
Because what Andrew *does* to this scenario is he
makes it safe.
I mean you're already happy…
Yay!
You'll go back to Andrew; we to each other and
what we'll have *achieved* in all this…

Touch wood…
(well sorry, not… 'touch wood'… I mean…)
is satisfying that question.
[–]
What it would be like.

MICHAEL   Okay…

RAFE   Okay as in you'll…
Do it?

MICHAEL   No just, okay as in… I register what you're
saying.

RAFE   Oh.
Sure.

MICHAEL   So what you're looking for…
Practically speaking?
Is like…

RAFE   A liaison.

MICHAEL   Right.

RAFE   A one-time thing.

MICHAEL   Forgetting about Andrew and just…

RAFE   Helping.

MICHAEL   You.

RAFE   Helping us.

MICHAEL   With your.

RAFE   Problem.

MICHAEL   Conundrum.

RAFE   That neither of us have ever even…

MICHAEL   Brushed.

RAFE   Another guy. Yeah.

MICHAEL   O. Kay.

RAFE   Okay as in… [*you'll do it*]?

MICHAEL   So it would just be us three?
            And we'd just like… have some fun?

RAFE   Erm.
            Well.
            We were thinking…

MICHAEL   Right.

RAFE   What we were actually thinking.

MICHAEL   Mm-hmm…

RAFE   We're looking for someone who can satisfy.
            Both of our urges.
            [–]
            Indi*vidually*.
            [–]
            So there's no.
            I don't know.
            'Messy issues.'
            Who looked at who.
            Who got more attention.
            All the things you read about, right?
            'Pros and cons'…
            [–]
            This proposal.
            (We feel.)
            Is a way round that.

MICHAEL   Okay.

RAFE   O. Kay.
            So.
            Michael.
            Just as a [*ballpark*]…
            What are you [*thinking*]?
            Your initial… [*thoughts*]?

MICHAEL   Well.
            I'm honoured.

Obviously.
That you feel we have a level of friendship that it
wouldn't cause any awkward scenes in Asda.

RAFE   [–]
            Sainsbury's.

MICHAEL   Yeah.
            And even though this is quite a... big thing...
            That you're suggesting.
            This... scenario?

RAFE   Scenario... yes...

MICHAEL   I mean...
            In theory...
            I'm... [*up for it*]
            Would I have to do it one after the other?
            Because I'm not sure how that would work.
            (Anatomically, right.)

RAFE   Oh no.

MICHAEL   No?

RAFE   Whatever you like.
            One one night...
            One the next.
            Over a weekend.
            A week apart.
            We haven't really given this much thought.

MICHAEL   No...

RAFE   Not really, no.

MICHAEL   And after it's happened.
            This evening or whatever.
            It's.
            Just a once thing, right?

RAFE   Once. Yes.
            Never again.
            Just to see what it's like.

MICHAEL   Okay.
           (I mean okay as in I get it.)
           One time only.
           One at a time.
           One night after the other.

RAFE   If that's what you'd [*prefer*]...
           Yeah.

MICHAEL   And.
           Andrew?

RAFE   Andrew?

MICHAEL   Does he [*come in to this*]... anywhere?
           Come in to this?

RAFE   Right.
           Well this is where we sort of have a condition.

MICHAEL   Right.

RAFE   Not that we've given this too much thought.

MICHAEL   Mm-hmm.

RAFE   We would like this to remain one hundred per cent
           between *us*.
           A *secret*.
           I mean.
           Were Andrew to even vaguely suspect.
           That could.
           Oh I don't know.
           That could cause all sorts of problems.

MICHAEL   In the cereal aisle.

RAFE   Exactly.
           We'd like to preserve the *perception* (right?)
           That we're happy and...
           Monogamous.
           (Which of course we are, but.)
           [–]
           Yeah.

	That we're happy. This really is so we can. Put to bed…
MICHAEL	('touch wood')
RAFE	Any sort of straying or. Temptations. That come with this length of relationship. Seven-and-a-half *years*. Does that make sense?
MICHAEL	Yes.
RAFE	Great.
MICHAEL	[–] Are you… Were you wanting us to start all this …tonight?
RAFE	No… No…
MICHAEL	Cos, like. Although I think in *theory* I'm up for it. I'd sort of like to sleep on it.
RAFE	Sure.
MICHAEL	Alone that is.
RAFE	Of course. Think about it. Please. I mean, our advice would be: (if you wanted our advice…) Don't think about Andrew. Andrew could really confuse things. We'd hate for him to get hurt by this. This really is just a favour between friends.
MICHAEL	Okay then…

RAFE   [–]

MICHAEL   I'll.
            Think about it.

RAFE   Great.
            G.
            -reat.

MICHAEL   Just one final [*question*]…

RAFE   Sure…

MICHAEL   Sorry.
            It's just.
            [–]
            Pete, I mean.
            [–]
            You've not [*said anything*]…
            The whole time.
            What do you.
            I mean.
            What do you think about all this?

RAFE   Well.
            [–]
            Actually…

PETE   It was my idea.

Two

MICHAEL *and* ANDREW.

ANDREW   Wow.
          I mean.

MICHAEL   Yeah.

ANDREW   That's a real.

MICHAEL   I know.

ANDREW   A really unusual…

MICHAEL   Tell me about it.

ANDREW   To put you in that position.

MICHAEL   Right.

ANDREW   And it would just be…

MICHAEL   …just be once.

ANDREW   With each of them?

MICHAEL   That's it.

ANDREW   Like, one after the other?

MICHAEL   That's what I couldn't work out.

ANDREW   But why?

MICHAEL   Because of my erection.
          You know.
          I'd have only just / *come*.

ANDREW   No why this a*rrange*ment?

MICHAEL   Oh.

ANDREW   Are they unhappy?

MICHAEL   I'm not sure.

ANDREW   Or just out*rageously* horny?

MICHAEL   I don't know.

ANDREW   Because it's interesting, isn't it?
           The logic of it all.
           Seven years?

MICHAEL   Seven-and-a-half.

ANDREW   And never in that time?
           Not even like a.

MICHAEL   Nothing.
           They *say*.

ANDREW   Well.
           Whatever floats your boat.
           (or in their case like a… two-man kayak…
           bobbing along…)
           I mean, they are a good match, aren't they?
           'Rafe and Pete.'
           It sort of goes together:
           The way it feels in the mouth.
           'You going to RafeandPete's?'
           'Yeah I'll see you at RafeandPete's.'
           'Sorted'.
           'Great – I'll see you at RafeandPete's.'

MICHAEL   Do you think we're *friends* of theirs, though?
           Good friends, I mean?

ANDREW   I dunno, I'm not sure.

MICHAEL   I mean they're *your* friends.

ANDREW   Yeah but..

MICHAEL   …we see them at parties and stuff…
           Facebook things.
           Mightn't it be weird?
           Like, crossing that line…

ANDREW   Well we're not like the *best* of friends or anything.
           They're just guys from uni, you know…
           We don't *holiday* together.

MICHAEL   Do you think it might affect us though?

ANDREW   Us?

MICHAEL   You and me.

ANDREW   [–]
I guess you have to see it from their point of view.
We've sort of been around the block, haven't we?
I feel like we ought to like…
Divvy ours up.
Give them a few.
Cos we've slept with like. What…

MICHAEL   You don't have to…

ANDREW   Between us though.

MICHAEL   …count or anything.

ANDREW   [–]
And it was Pete's idea?

MICHAEL   Apparently.

ANDREW   That's interesting.

MICHAEL   Really?

ANDREW   Yeah.

MICHAEL   Why?

ANDREW   Just is.

MICHAEL   [–]
So what do you…?
You know.

ANDREW   Well.

MICHAEL   Cos you're not supposed to know.
[–]
That was one of their conditions.

ANDREW   Really?

MICHAEL   Yeah.

ANDREW   Why?

MICHAEL   Well, it's embarrassing I guess.

ANDREW   Yeah I suppose.

MICHAEL   It's not something you'd want to go around
            advertising is it?

ANDREW   True.

MICHAEL   And if you don't think it's cool then I'd totally
            understand.

ANDREW   No, I'm glad you told me.

MICHAEL   Really?

ANDREW   Yeah of course.
            It's just...
            If it's going to be The End...
            If they're looking for a *reason*.
            This could *be* that reason.

MICHAEL   I know.

ANDREW   And then it gets messy.

MICHAEL   Yeah.

ANDREW   You the *named* party.

MICHAEL   But wouldn't it get awkward?

ANDREW   Well...

MICHAEL   In Asda?
            You know.
            (Sainsbury's, whatever.)

ANDREW   As long as you're sure it isn't anything deeper
            then...
            [–]

MICHAEL   I mean, this is how we do things, right?
            For us to work.
            Isn't it?

ANDREW   Yeah, of course.

MICHAEL   And does it still work for you?
            Our arrangement?

ANDREW   I mean it goes against one of our rules:
            'Someone we both know.'

MICHAEL   But on this occasion?

ANDREW   [–]
            Sure.

MICHAEL   I just think it'd really help them out.
            For their like… sanity and pride.

ANDREW   I mean I just can't *imagine*.
            Have they ever even seen another [*dick*]…?

MICHAEL   Well they must have watched porn.

ANDREW   Well obviously, of course.
            Everyone's watched porn.
            (My nan's watched porn.)
            I'm talking about right up close…
            There in the flesh.
            It's going to be some big.
            (I don't know…)
            Surprise.
            Have you talked about.
            Roles?
            Who goes where?

MICHAEL   No.
            We didn't really get that far.
            Should I [*talk about it*]…?
            Or should I just [*wait*].
            No, I guess not.

ANDREW   Are you excited?

MICHAEL   I'm not sure.

ANDREW   They're very good-looking.

MICHAEL   They're okay.

ANDREW   Come on, it's alright.
          You don't have to…

MICHAEL   What?

ANDREW   Bottle up your excitement.

MICHAEL   Honestly…?
          Excitement?

ANDREW   Yeah!
          Rafe and Pete are cute.

MICHAEL   Really?

ANDREW   Rafe and Pete are definitely cute.
          [–]
          I'm jealous if I'm honest.
          [–]
          Seven-and-a-half years.
          That's a very long time.

MICHAEL   Yeah, I suppose it is.

ANDREW   Look.
          Michael.
          Just. Go with it. Okay?
          Enjoy it.
          I don't mind.
          Go.
          With.
          'The flow.'

Three

MICHAEL *and* PETE.

PETE   The thing is Michael:
            There are some things Rafe won't try.

MICHAEL   Okay.

PETE   Things he doesn't even *try* to *enjoy*.
            So if this is going to be a one-time thing.
            That's what I wanna do.
            [–]
            The things that Rafe won't do.

MICHAEL   Right.

PETE   Hang on a sec – you probably think I'm talking
            about *pissing* or something.
            'Scat love.'
            Nooo.
            No…
            That's not what I want at all.
            It's just like.
            Basic bedroom stuff.
            Tying each other up.
            Being a bit rough.
            You know;
            Normal adult behaviour.
            Because Rafe's quite a gentle soul.
            (I'm sure that hasn't escaped you)
            Sometimes I just want him to grab my hair…
            Throw me around a bit.
            Slap me.
            I mean some people talk about wax? Like…
            dripping candle wax?
            Have you ever done that?
            [–]
            Shit, sorry.
            I didn't mean to pry.

MICHAEL   We can be rough.

PETE   Really?

MICHAEL   Yeah.
            Look this is your night…
            So if wax or…
            Clamps.

PETE   Clamps?

MICHAEL   Well if clamps are.

PETE   Well I didn't think about clamps.
            Should I think about clamps?

MICHAEL   Yeah, if you want.

PETE   You mean nipple clamps right?

MICHAEL   It was only a suggestion.
            I was actually going to say handcuffs.
            But. Clamps was what came out.

PETE   Yeah.
            No, of course.
            And the wax thing?
            How does that sound…?

MICHAEL   …weird…
            (sure)
            But I don't see why not.
            If I'm honest it's quite hot.

PETE   Really?

MICHAEL   Yeah.
            Definitely.

PETE   Great.
            Good.
            I'll get on it then I guess.
            'Yankee Candle go.'

MICHAEL   Okay.

PETE   And… rough stuff…
            Aggression?

MICHAEL   Rough stuff's fine.

PETE   I mean I don't want a Nazi costume or anything.

MICHAEL   No.

PETE   Although if I only have a day.

MICHAEL   A day?

PETE   Evening, whatever.
(Although whatever it is, we should both have equal time.
Rafe'll get really funny if we don't.)
But like, when you start to kiss me maybe if you like…

MICHAEL   Wait.
Hold on.
Who said anything about kissing?

PETE   Of course we're going to kiss.

MICHAEL   Prostitutes don't kiss.

PETE   You're not a prostitute.
You're a friend.

MICHAEL   Yeah but.
I've got to save something for Andrew.

PETE   No but it's just standard, right?

MICHAEL   Not really.

PETE   It's not?

MICHAEL   No.

PETE   Well.
More fool me.
Guess I'm just not *used* to all this…
(etiquette and stuff.)

MICHAEL   No?

PETE   Do you normally?

MICHAEL   What?

PETE   Kiss?

MICHAEL   Andrew?

PETE   Other guys.
            [–]
            Cos you do that, right?
            The two of you...?
            [–]
            Sorry, I shouldn't pry.

MICHAEL   Look, I'll think about kissing.

PETE   I just wouldn't know what to do with my face.
            Turn to the side?
            I don't know...
            Wear a.

MICHAEL   Mask.

PETE   A mask?

MICHAEL   Like, a gimp mask.
            If you want.

PETE   Really?

MICHAEL   Put a ball in your mouth?

PETE   [–]

MICHAEL   They're just ideas.

PETE   Sure.

MICHAEL   I mean, I'm not saying that I, personally.

PETE   Look, that's not the point of this exercise...
            To spy on you.

MICHAEL   No, but...

PETE   What you and Andrew get up to in your own
            time is...

MICHAEL   Honestly Pete, it's fine.

PETE   I just want you to think about the kissing thing.

MICHAEL   Sure.

PETE   Maybe you could like.
            Bite me a bit?
            Throw me around.

MICHAEL   I'll think about it.

PETE   Cool.
            Okay, great.
            Think about it, yeah.
            Have a bit of a think.

Four

MICHAEL *and* RAFE.

RAFE   I want to be treated gently.
            Like.
            Really looked after.
            Romantically.
            Sensually…
            Kissing me all over…

MICHAEL   Sensually?

RAFE   Yeah.

MICHAEL   You make it sound like we're selling soap.

RAFE   No just…
            Candles and incense.
            Massage oil perhaps.
            I think that's what I'd like.
            From doing all this.
            Cos it's not so much the sex.
            (I mean of course I want the sex.)
            (That's the whole point.)
            But I want it to be about the experience as well.
            Things the other doesn't get from the other.

MICHAEL   Right.

RAFE   You know sometimes I think a rent boy would
have been easier.
We'd know what we were getting.
I mean you might not even be good in bed.

MICHAEL   Thanks.

RAFE   Maybe *I'm* not good in bed.
Perhaps you could tell me?

MICHAEL   You want me to tell you if you're bad in bed?

RAFE   Maybe.
I don't know.
(It could be where we're going wrong)
I just want you to make me feel special, that's all.

MICHAEL   You see I'm.
(Really.)
Okay with all this.
Honestly, I am.
It's just.
What I don't want to happen is.
All these revelations about the other person.
Because now I have this image of what Pete does
or doesn't do.
And.
What you've proposed is fine but.
I can't have all this *intimate detail*.

RAFE   Pete just wants to get fucked.
Doesn't he.
To slap him around and.
Shit on him.
Right?

MICHAEL   Rafe.
Come on.
That's what I'm talking about.

RAFE   Well... is it true?

MICHAEL   I can't get involved in that kind of thing.

RAFE   Why not?

MICHAEL   Because then it becomes about a problem.

RAFE   There is no problem.

MICHAEL   No, I know there's not a problem but…

RAFE   There *is* no problem.

MICHAEL   Then…
            All these little *meetings*…
            (Pete and I…)
            (*This*…)
            They weren't exactly the *best* idea, were they?

RAFE   We're just having a drink, right?

MICHAEL   I know but…

RAFE   Can't friends have a drink?

MICHAEL   Yes… They can but…
            When have we ever done that?

RAFE   We could… perhaps…
            Two contemporaries maybe?

MICHAEL   'Contemporaries.'

RAFE   Sure.
            Networking perhaps?

MICHAEL   You think that's what we are?

RAFE   Well we both work nearby.
            Our work's not dissimilar.
            It might be useful.

MICHAEL   What, hooking up?
            Yeah, pitch that to your boss…
            See how that goes down.

RAFE   [–]
            You're not thinking of pulling out?

MICHAEL   No, look, I'm fine with it.
            Really.

I'm actually looking forward to it.
Though part of me's like, let's just down this
fucking beer and get the fuck on with it.
You know?
I worry you're pinning too much on this.
That you're wanting something else.
[–]
This isn't going to save you.
If that's what you think.

RAFE   I just want a bit of massage oil.
That's all.
[–]
I don't want *saving*.
I'm not *drowning*.
Just…
Candles and some oil.
[–]
To be treated really nice.

Five

RAFE, PETE *and* MICHAEL.

PETE   Well.

RAFE   Yeah.

MICHAEL   Here we go.

PETE   Here we…
Go.

RAFE   Are you…
Okay?

MICHAEL   Yes.
Thanks.
Are you?

RAFE   Yes.
            Yeah.
            Aren't we?

PETE   Yep.

            [–]

RAFE   So… I won the toss.

MICHAEL   You tossed a *coin*?

RAFE   So there were no accusations or.

MICHAEL   Fine.

RAFE   So it's fair.
            So Pete is going to go to…

PETE   …my sister lives nearby.
            We're going to get Chinese.
            I think she's got a film.

RAFE   LoveFilm.

PETE   What?

RAFE   Your sister has LoveFilm.

PETE   Yeah.

RAFE   So it's probably from there.

PETE   [–]
            We have Netflix.

MICHAEL   Right.

PETE   I didn't actually know LoveFilm was a thing any
            more.

            [–]

            So anyway.

RAFE   Yes.

PETE   I'll be back around…

RAFE   Eleven. At eleven.
            Is eleven okay with you?

MICHAEL   Eleven is.
            Yeah.
            (I thought you'd be.
            Gone actually.)
            (Whichever one it was.)
            (But.)
            Eleven o'clock is great.

RAFE   Great.

PETE   Well.
            Erm.
            Have fun.

RAFE   Thanks.
            You too.
            With your.

PETE   Yeah.
            [–]

RAFE   See you later.

            PETE *exits*.

            Well.
            So.
            Come in.
            Make yourself…
            I mean.
            However you want to make yourself.

MICHAEL   Thanks.

RAFE   [–]
            You, erm.
            [–]
            You look nice.

MICHAEL   Thanks.
            [–]
            You too.

RAFE   Did you go to the gym today?

MICHAEL   Yeah.

RAFE   You've got that like.
            Pumped look.

MICHAEL   Thanks.
            I went about four.

RAFE   Right.
            Was that for tonight or…

MICHAEL   Just. Convenient.
            I guess. But…
            Yeah, I suppose.

RAFE   Well thank you.
            I like that.

MICHAEL   I went swimming as well.

RAFE   Swimming *and* the gym?

MICHAEL   Yeah.

RAFE   Impressive.

MICHAEL   So maybe that's why.
            They say it in *Men's Health* actually.
            (Well, that's what they advise.)
            Before you go on dates.
            A last-minute session.

RAFE   You think this is a date?

MICHAEL   No.

RAFE   I've never been on a date.

MICHAEL   Never?

RAFE   No.

MICHAEL   Wow.

RAFE   [–]
            Your T-shirt smells like it's just come out the dryer.

MICHAEL   It has.

RAFE   Is it Bold you use…?

MICHAEL   I don't know.

RAFE   It smells like ours.

MICHAEL   It's, erm. Lavender or something.
            I don't actually do the washing in our house.

RAFE   You made an effort though.
            Thank you.
            You look really great.

MICHAEL   It's just a clean T-shirt…

RAFE   You always look great.

MICHAEL   [–]
            You look good too.

RAFE   Thanks.

MICHAEL   (I cook, instead)
            (just in case you think I'm like…)

RAFE   We should probably have something to drink.

MICHAEL   Yes.

RAFE   What would you like?

MICHAEL   Beer?

RAFE   I could make a G and T.
            We haven't got long so.
            I could make it really strong.

MICHAEL   That'd be great.

RAFE   And that way we won't have like.
            [–]

MICHAEL   What?

RAFE   It sounds really stupid but.
            We won't have full bladders.

MICHAEL   Right…

RAFE   Sometimes, we'll go out and.
         We'll drink loads of beer.
         (Pints.)
         And we'll come back and we'll be [*having sex*].
         And all I want to do is pee.

MICHAEL   Some people like that.

RAFE   [–]

MICHAEL   On the internet.
         People pay.

RAFE   People pay for anything on the internet.

MICHAEL   They do.
         Yeah.

RAFE   [–]
         Gin.

MICHAEL   Sure.

         [–]

         Nice flat…

RAFE   Yeah.
         We're lucky with it actually.
         We've got two bedrooms.
         So our parents can stay or.
         Friends can crash.

MICHAEL   I think we should get our own place.
         Andrew and I.

RAFE   Who do you live with?

MICHAEL   Oh, just these girls.
         I mean, don't get me wrong, they're very nice and
         all that…
         But they're *single* girls, you know.
         They like doing single-girl *things*.

Like googling Ryan Gosling.
But one-beds are so much.
It's a bit of a step up.
I mean, we'll do it at some point but.
Just for now?
It sort of makes sense.
Financially.

RAFE   Yeah.

MICHAEL   You okay?
            Rafe?

RAFE   Yeah, yeah, no [*it's nothing*].

MICHAEL   Honestly?

RAFE   It's just.
            We probably shouldn't…

MICHAEL   What?

RAFE   Talk about [*our partners*].
            Let's just.
            I dunno.
            Let's. Erm.
            [–]
            This is really weird.

MICHAEL   I know.

RAFE   I don't really know how we…
            Start this…

MICHAEL   No.

RAFE   I don't know what I expected…
            Like… a smoke screen or something.
            'Tonight Matthew I'm going to be…'

MICHAEL   Fucked?

RAFE   [–]

MICHAEL   Sorry.

RAFE   Should we maybe…
              Start again.
              Michael?
              Can we start all this again?

MICHAEL   Okay.

RAFE   Yeah, I think that's what we should do.
              Let's start all this again.

Six

ANDREW.

ANDREW   Hey Rafe
              (and Pete…
              …of course).
              Michael and I were just saying how it's been ages
              since we've seen you guys.
              So. Do you fancy dinner sometime or.
              Drinks somewhere?
              Anyway. Call me back.
              We're free all weekend so.
              Speak to you soon.
              Oh, it's.
              Andrew.
              By the way.

Seven

RAFE *and* PETE.

        [–]

ANDREW   *Anyway. Call me back.*
              We're free all weekend so.
              Speak to you soon.
              Oh, it's.
              Andrew.
              By the way.

        [–]

PETE   It could just be odd timing.

RAFE   No.

PETE   A massive coincidence.

RAFE   No way.
           Honestly.
           He knows.

PETE   Maybe last night.
           When Michael went out.
           He just. Went through Facebook or.
           Thought about who they hadn't seen in a while and.
           Landed on us.

RAFE   I don't buy it.
           Sorry.
           '*Oh it's… Andrew*'?
           I'm not buying that at all.

PETE   Well what are you going to do?
           Call him up and say: 'How dare you call me?'
           Even if he knows…
           'How dare you call me up.'
           I mean, come on… really?

RAFE   Well what do we do?

PETE   Just text him.

RAFE   Text him?

PETE   Yeah, like 'Hey, sounds good, when were you thinking?'

RAFE   [–]
              Okay.

PETE   It's not hard, is it?

RAFE   Fine.

PETE   And then call Michael, and ask him if he knows.

RAFE   Me?

PETE   Yeah.

RAFE   *I* should call him?

PETE   Yes.

RAFE   Why me?

PETE   Well you slept with him.

RAFE   [–]
              Really?

PETE   Well yeah.

RAFE   *Seriously…?*

PETE   Just text him, Rafe.
              For fuck's sake.

RAFE   Cos *I* slept with him?

PETE   Yes.
              You've got a link now.

RAFE   (Fine.)
              'Hey Andrew.
              Thanks for your… voicemail.'

PETE   No, no, no. 'Good to hear from you.'

RAFE   'Good.
              To.
              Hear from you.'

PETE   Because then it's like…
         It's good to hear from him.

RAFE   [–]
         'Dinner sounds good. When's good
         for
         you?'

PETE   Read it back.

RAFE   'Hey Andrew. Good to hear from you. Dinner
         sounds good. When's good for you?'

PETE   You've put good three times.

RAFE   Sent.

PETE   …guess it doesn't matter.

         [–]

RAFE   Do you think that he's cross?
         That he's like…
         Hit him or something?

PETE   Andrew?
         Hit someone?

RAFE   I mean, last night, when he went home, maybe
         Andrew suspected where Michael *was* or
         something.
         Smelt alcohol on his breath.

PETE   Was he drunk?

RAFE   We'd had drinks.

PETE   You weren't drunk.
         Were you?

RAFE   I'd had a couple.

PETE   Exactly.
         So why would he be drunk?

RAFE   Look… we said we wouldn't [*talk about this*].
         Didn't we?

PETE   Fine.

RAFE   What happens in Vegas.

PETE   Sure.

RAFE   Don't make a big / deal.

PETE   I'm not.

RAFE   Good then.
          Because.
          [–]

PETE   What?
          Because what?

RAFE   We tossed a coin. Didn't we?
          I won the toss and.
          I'm *sorry* for going first.
          But don't make me feel bad about it.

PETE   I'm not making you feel bad.

RAFE   Perhaps this whole thing was just a really
          bad idea.

PETE   What?

RAFE   Maybe we should just, like…

PETE   You're not pulling out.

RAFE   I didn't say I'm pulling out.

PETE   We're not pulling out.
          [–]
          You can't just do that.
          I haven't had my turn.

RAFE   [–]
          And what about after the turn?

PETE   What?

RAFE   What are you going to do then?
          In a couple of months' time.
          Find another friend?

PETE	Why are you putting this on me?
RAFE	It's just a question.
PETE	What are *you* going to do?
RAFE	It wasn't my idea.
PETE	[–] I guess we'll just do the same we do now.
RAFE	And beyond that? For the rest of our lives?
PETE	*What?*
RAFE	What do you see then?
PETE	I don't see anything, Rafe. I'm not a mind-reader, am I? I'm not Mystic fucking Meg.
RAFE	I just want to know where you see us going.
PETE	Where's this come from?
RAFE	[–] Where do you think?
PETE	[–] Okay fine. [–] I'm in a very classy backless dress. With a white-lace gown. Six bridesmaids and a train.
RAFE	Pete.
PETE	Is that what you wanna hear?
RAFE	No, don't be a dick.
PETE	[–] You on the other hand, are in… A Hugo Boss suit… Jermyn Street shirt and a Paul Smith tie. (that blue one you like with the little white dots.) [–]

And our mums have gone and bought exactly the
same dress…
(I'm guessing M&S)
And so they're having a little bitch-off about who
looks the best.
(Cos my mum's got a hat and your mum's got one
of those like fascinator things.)
(It's all become very political.)
And my dad's complaining cos he hates anything
formal and your dad's loving it cos deep down,
let's face it, he paid for it all.

RAFE   No he did not!

PETE   Well in my future he did.
Cos we've hired that house, you know.
The one we passed on the coast?
(We wanted to do it properly so…)
We stay in separate rooms;
You with Tara, me with Sophie.
We've all gone and had those like… face masks
and shit.
Plucking our eyebrows.
That sort of thing.
(we sort of look ridiculous but also kind of cute)
And Tara makes you some sort of cucumber
smoothie…
(to 'cleanse out your liver' or whatever you think
it does)
And I sit next door with a packet of Marlboro
Lights cos I *know* I don't smoke any more but I'm
really fucking nervous about my speech, *okay*?
(Although I don't need to worry cos obviously it's
amazing…)
And down in the foyer all of our friends are
looking really bloody classy.
(Except Gracie, of course, she's the same old
mess.)
(she hasn't even washed her hair)
(…what do you expect?)

But the rest of them are all like ridiculously
excited cos it's their first *gay wedding* and they've
all been like posting it on Facebook and. Telling
all their colleagues.
Not that we're pandering to that.
Absolutely not.
There's no pink champagne…
No *disco classics* as we walk down the aisle.
Kylie is banned.
This is a classy affair.
Veuve Clicquot.
Wine from Waitrose.
Enya.

RAFE   Enya?

PETE   Yeah…
Just to like, set the mood.
[–]
And without being funny, the whole day is
basically…
[–]
In a word…
[–]
Perfect.
[–]
In that really clichéd Hollywood way;
– The rain stays off.
– The grass is *freshly mown*.
– And everyone leaves going 'Yeah, they're
classy.'
'They are really classy guys.'
[–]
Because everything's been great.
[–]
Amazing you might say.

[–]

RAFE   And does my mum win?

PETE   What?

RAFE   The bitch-off?

PETE   Course.

RAFE   That's good.

PETE   She's got my mum in a headlock.
         They're falling over waiters serving 'miniature
         fish and chips'.

RAFE   [–]
         Do I still have my hair?

PETE   Yep.

RAFE   Well that's a relief.

PETE   You're looking really good actually.

RAFE   How old are we?

PETE   [–]
         Don't know.

         [–]

RAFE   Do you think we should get a dog?

PETE   You don't want a dog.

RAFE   We could.

PETE   You have to want a dog, Rafe.
         It isn't a solution.

         [–]

RAFE   We *could* get a dog.
         A little terrier, perhaps?

         [–]

Eight

PETE *and* MICHAEL.

PETE   Thank you.

MICHAEL   For what?

PETE   Doing this.

MICHAEL   It's fine.

PETE   I mean I know it's a bit seedy but…

MICHAEL   Pete.
           Come on.
           I just…
           Want this to be fun.

PETE   Sure.

MICHAEL   What's happening right now is that it's occupying
           time.
           Rafe always sending me these pissy little texts.
           And that? For my job?
           It's really not good.

PETE   Sorry.

MICHAEL   It's fine.
           [–]
           Did you buy any candles?

PETE   Yeah. I bought…
           Well here, I got a few things actually.

           [–]

MICHAEL   Interesting…
           Peter.

PETE   Don't call me Peter.
           My dad calls me Peter.

MICHAEL   I think we can have some fun with this.

PETE   So like.
           How do you want to start?

MICHAEL   Well your T-shirt would be a good place.

PETE   Really?
          Straight in?

MICHAEL   I thought you wanted someone to take charge
          of you.

PETE   I do…

MICHAEL   Then TAKE OFF YOUR FUCKING T-SHIRT.

PETE   (oh my God)
          (Michael!)

MICHAEL   Now I want you to sit on this chair.
          Sit on the fucking chair.
          Hands behind your back.
          [–]
          That's it.
          [–]
          And now…
          Peter Mitchell.
          Do you know what we're going to have?
          [–]

PETE   Sex?

MICHAEL   Fun.
          We're going to have some fucking fun.

Nine

ANDREW.

ANDREW   Hey it's me.
          Just thought I'd check in…
          You know.
          See where you are.
          Dead perhaps or…
          At the gym…?
          (I'm guessing one of the two…)
          [–]
          I'm… About to cook dinner, so…
          Do you want me to leave you some…?
          I was gonna do this like Thai prawn-stir-fry
          thing…
          (I got it out the *Metro* actually.)
          It's like…
          Prawns… (obviously.)
          Carrot… onion…
          'A tablespoon of garlic paste'
          Spinach (for Popeye)
          And…
          [–]
          Noodles.
          Not rice.
          (*Controversial.*)
          [–]
          Anyway. I don't know if it'll keep; that's the only
          thing…
          What with it being… seafood and all that.
          (I don't want anyone getting the shits in the
          night.)
          [–]
          Well, I hope you're having fun…
          (Wherever you may be.)
          Maybe give me a call sometime.
          'ET phone home'
          [–]
          Love you (*et cetera*).

Let me know about those prawns, okay?
[–]
Yeah, just…
Let me know.

Ten

RAFE *and* PETE.

RAFE   So.

PETE   Yeah.

RAFE   *So.*

PETE   Mm-hmm.

RAFE   Out of our.

PETE   Yeah.

RAFE   Systems.
[–]
Done.
Dusted.
Under the.
Carpet.

PETE   Yes.

RAFE   One time only.
One time and it's…

PETE   Yeah.

RAFE   …over and out.

[–]

Did you.
Did you.
Enjoy the whole.

PETE   Rafe.

RAFE   Sorry.

PETE   Didn't we?

RAFE   Yeah.

PETE   So I think we should just.

RAFE   Fine okay.

            [–]

            Is it though, Pete?

PETE   What?

RAFE   Out of our systems?

PETE   Rafe.
            Seriously.
            Why are you…

RAFE   Is it?

PETE   Yes.

RAFE   And after all this.
            You still love me, right?

PETE   Fucking hell.

RAFE   Just to be sure.

PETE   Yes. I love you.

RAFE   Okay then.
            [–]
            Okay.

Eleven

ANDREW, RAFE *and* PETE.

ANDREW   Rafe.
          Pete.
          It's.
          Great to see you guys.
          Thanks for coming over.

RAFE   No, thanks for having us.

ANDREW   I'm sorry we're not cooking…

RAFE   No, no.

PETE   That's fine.

ANDREW   I know it's lazy but…

RAFE   No, not at all.

ANDREW   [–]
          Thanks for this.

PETE   We weren't sure what you both…

ANDREW   No prosecco's great, thank you.
          'Classy.'
          [–]
          Please; take a seat.

RAFE   Thanks.

ANDREW   *So.*
          How are you both?

RAFE   Er.
          Well… thank you.
          Yes.

ANDREW   Haven't seen you guys in ages.

RAFE   No?

ANDREW   Can't even remember when.
          You look well.

RAFE   Thank you.
                You?
                Are you well?

ANDREW   Oh, yeah…
                I'm great.
                Very good.

RAFE   Great.

PETE   This is nice. [*The flat.*]

ANDREW   You've been here before, right?

PETE   No I don't think we have.

ANDREW   Oh right, well…
                The girls are away so…
                Hurrah!
                Freedom at last…

RAFE   Jennifer Walker's party.

ANDREW   Sorry?

RAFE   That's when we last saw you.

ANDREW   Oh, 'Jenny *Gregor*'.

PETE   (Whatever she calls herself these days.)

ANDREW   *Teachers*…

PETE   I know, right?

ANDREW   I almost deleted her.

RAFE   (Who's Jenny Gregor?)

ANDREW   Apparently it's her mum's maiden name.
                So the kids can't find her.

PETE   (Jennifer Walker.)

RAFE   (Oh.)

ANDREW   Like the kids'd want to.
                (Dozy bitch.)

RAFE   Well anyway, that was it.
            Jennifer Jenny Walker Gregor's party.

ANDREW   We must have seen you since though.

RAFE   No.

ANDREW   Did we not... bump in to you?
            Yeah at Cineworld...

RAFE   Oh, yes...

ANDREW   Pete had forgotten his glasses.

PETE   Ah... good memory.

RAFE   He always forgets his glasses.

PETE   And then they make you pay and you're like
            'They're in my bedside drawer!! Clearly I meant
            to bring them...'

ANDREW   No, it has been a long time...
            [–]
            We must work harder.
            [–]
            See each other more.

RAFE   Yeah, absolutely.

ANDREW   So... what have you both been up to?

RAFE   Oh...
            Nothing much.
            You know...
            Work.
            Play.
            Same as ever.
            Work and play.

ANDREW   Anything fun?

RAFE   Work or...?

ANDREW   Either...

RAFE   No...
            [–]

Nothing much.
How about you?
Anything… fun?

ANDREW   I lead a very *boring* life these days.
           Very routine.

RAFE   Yeah…

ANDREW   No *liaisons* for me.

RAFE   (…no?)

ANDREW   [–]
           Oh I did get to go to Glasgow for a conference.
           Three days in a Novotel.
           Got pissed in the bar on cheap champagne.
           That's about the height of it.

PETE   On the taxpayer…

ANDREW   Hardly.

PETE   Is that not… frowned upon?

ANDREW   Oh no, *I* bought the champagne.

PETE   Oh.

ANDREW   That's why it was cheap.
           And it was Glasgow so like…
           Five pounds.
           [–]
           Come on guys;
           There must be some goss, surely?

RAFE   No… not really…

ANDREW   You're usually always full of it.

RAFE   Are we?

ANDREW   Who's been seeing so-and-so, and so-and-so, and
           so-and-so…

PETE   I think we're getting a bit old for all that.

ANDREW   Are we?

PETE   Perhaps.

ANDREW   I hope not.
            [–]
            Didn't I see you with a dog the other day?

RAFE   A dog?

ANDREW   On Facebook.

RAFE   Oh… yeah…

ANDREW   You haven't got a dog, have you?

PETE   No, it's my grandma's.

RAFE   A Labradoodle.

ANDREW   A what…?

RAFE   I know.

PETE   It's a Labrador-poodle cross.

ANDREW   Wow.
            Are you joking?
            That's actually a thing?

RAFE   I thought that as well.
            I mean some sick breeder must have done that,
            right?

PETE   She wants us to have a puppy.

ANDREW   She's going to breed them?

PETE   Yeah.
            They're worth a lot of money.

ANDREW   She should breed it with a chihuahua.
            See what comes out.

PETE   I'd pay to see that.

ANDREW   Are you going to get one then?

PETE   [–]
            Erm.

RAFE   Well.

PETE   I'd love to get one... but...

RAFE   It's something we're thinking about.

ANDREW   Okay.

RAFE   The logistics of it all.

ANDREW   Sure.

PETE   We're both out during the day so...

RAFE   Is Michael home, Andrew or...?

ANDREW   [–]
            He's just at the shops.
            [–]
            We... ran out of ice...

RAFE   Right.

ANDREW   Tonic as well.
            Crisps...
            Dips.
            (Pringles, whatever.)

PETE   Sounds like quite a list.

ANDREW   Oh, he's always so slow.
            He'll have totally lost track of time.
            Popped into Starbucks or.
            Bumped in to a friend.
            It really annoys me actually; he's so *elusive*
            sometimes.

RAFE   It's easily done.

ANDREW   Which one of you's the slow one?

PETE   Rafe is.

ANDREW   You are?

PETE   He flosses his teeth.

ANDREW   Oh, good.

PETE   And then: 'I have to take my contacts out'
            'I need to wash my face'
            'I've got to check the door.'

RAFE   (Leave it Pete.)

PETE   You do.

ANDREW   Check the door?

PETE   Thank you.

RAFE   It's normal to check the door, Pete.

PETE   Not five times.
            What are you checking?

RAFE   I'm checking that it's locked.

PETE   Of course it's locked.

RAFE   *Okay.*

PETE   (We have a latch on the door.)

RAFE   Well I'm just making *sure*.

PETE   Why? You know it's locked.

ANDREW   It wasn't supposed to be a like, can of worms or
            anything…

            [–]

            Actually guys, I'm…
            …sort of glad I've got you by myself if I'm
            honest.

RAFE   Really?

ANDREW   Yeah…
            [–]
            There's, erm.
            There's something I wanted to talk to you about.
            Before Michael gets back.
            (Privately.
            If you don't mind.)

RAFE   Sure.
            Okay…

ANDREW   It's something a bit.
            Personal.

RAFE   Right.

ANDREW   Sensitive.

RAFE   Mm-hmm.

ANDREW   I hope you don't mind?

RAFE   No.
            Go a… head.

ANDREW   (God my palms have gone sweaty…)

PETE   (Are you okay, Andrew?)

ANDREW   (Yeah it's just…)
            [–]
            I hope you don't think I'm speaking out of turn but.
            This is sort of very awkward for me to talk about.
            I don't want us to like… fall out or anything.
            But.
            Okay, I'm just going to say it.
            [–]
            Well…
            Michael and I have an open relationship.
            [–]
            Did you…
            Know that?

RAFE   No.

PETE   No…

RAFE   Nope.

PETE   Didn't know that, no.

ANDREW   Right.
            [–]
            Well we have a lot of rules.

Obviously.
To make sure it's okay.
Like: we're not allowed to see that person more
than once...
(That one's really important.)
(So there's no... attachment, I suppose)
Second, we don't talk about it.
(I mean usually we know.)
(It's sort of a sixth sense but.)
Finally...
The most important...
[–]
It can never be a friend.

RAFE   Right.
         We didn't know that.

ANDREW   Really?

RAFE   [–]
         No.
         About the... [open] relationship thing...

ANDREW   [–]
         You never suspected?

RAFE   Never crossed our minds.

ANDREW   Well people have needs, don't they?
         Behind closed doors.
         Urges.
         Pangs.
         'Hidden desires.'
         But the thing is, guys, there's something that's
         been on my mind a lot lately.
         Something I haven't *done*.
         And...
         (I'm pretty sure Michael *has*, you see.)

         [–]

         I've never had a threesome.

         [–]

RAFE   Oh.

PETE   Okay.

ANDREW   And I…
          (Christ this is really awkward)
          But…
          I wondered if…
          … you had…?

PETE   [–]
          No.

RAFE   No.

PETE   No.

RAFE   No way.

ANDREW   Because I know you're quite [*tight*].
          The two of you;
          Quite tight…
          I mean I remember you at uni…
          No one else got a look-in, did they?
          But I wondered if you maybe…
          Dabbled in that stuff?
          Privately, perhaps…

RAFE   [–]
          No.

ANDREW   No?

RAFE   Not at all, no.
          We're exclusive.
          Both of us.
          [–]
          We don't sleep with other people.

ANDREW   Really?

RAFE   Yeah.

ANDREW   *Really?*
          I mean, there's never been like an incident or…

RAFE   Nothing.

ANDREW   Never?

RAFE   Nope…
            [–]

ANDREW   It's just…
            It's funny, I guess.
            The two of you have that vibe.

RAFE   Really?

ANDREW   Yeah I mean.
            The way you look at me sometimes.
            The way you look at Michael.
            It's sort of a bit.
            [–]
            Pursuing.

RAFE   I just… think that's how we look.

ANDREW   So you mean to tell me that you've really never…

RAFE   No.

ANDREW   Not even like a snog…?

RAFE   We've never even brushed another guy.

ANDREW   But aren't you *curious* about it?
            What it would be like?
            That feeling of flesh on someone else's skin?
            [–]
            I mean…
            What I'm trying to say is…
            I'm…
            Offering this to you.

            [–]

RAFE   But it goes against your rule:
            Someone you both know.

ANDREW   Yeah I know.
            That's why it's… awkward.

But I want it to be *safe*.
I mean you're 'already happy', right?
So it wouldn't be a problem…
I mean I see a lot of couples on Grindr, of course,
but it sort of freaks me out; the idea of all that.
Like, did you see that documentary about Russia
recently?

RAFE   Yes! We did.
            We did, didn't we, Pete?

ANDREW   Well then you don't want to be that person, do you?
            Tortured and stuff.

RAFE   Of course not, no.

PETE   (You don't want to get knifed.)

ANDREW   I'm just trying to make it safe.
            For everyone, right?
            I mean we go way back, don't we?
            The three of us: good friends.
            It wouldn't cause us any *problems*, would it?
            If it was something we wanted to try perhaps?
            Spice things up…
            [–]
            I'd be the person you could do that with.

RAFE   [–]
            I think we're potentially getting into something
            I'm not sure we should necessarily be getting
            in to.
            [–]
            I hope you don't mind.

ANDREW   [–]
            Sure?

RAFE   Sure.

ANDREW   [–]
            Fair enough.
            [–]

Like I said: this was something that could
potentially have been very awkward between us so.
Let's move on.
Before it starts to get awkward.

RAFE   Thank you.

ANDREW   That's fine.
            Really, it's… fine.

            [–]

PETE   I think we should do it.

RAFE   (What?)

PETE   [–]
            Yeah, why not?

ANDREW   Wow.
            Erm…
            Really?

PETE   Andrew's right.
            We'd be lying if we said we weren't curious.

RAFE   (Pete.
            Come on.
            I don't think this is *appropriate*.)

PETE   (Why not?)

ANDREW   Look if the two of you don't fancy me…

PETE   No…
            Not at all…
            You're a very… handsome man, Andrew…

ANDREW   'Handsome.'
            (Very nineties.)

PETE   And like you say… you're a friend of ours,
            aren't you?

ANDREW   Exactly, yes.

PETE   So that would make it safe.
            For all of us. Right?

	The confidentiality. We couldn't ever tell anyone.
ANDREW	See, I like the way he thinks.
RAFE	(Pete, can we not…)
ANDREW	I mean what you don't know doesn't hurt you, right, Rafe?
RAFE	I'm not sure what you mean.
ANDREW	There must be a part of you that's curious, right? About what it would be like?
RAFE	I'm not curious. No.
ANDREW	You don't lie in bed at night and…

[–]

Think about what could have been?

[–]

MICHAEL *enters*.

MICHAEL	Hey.
RAFE *and* PETE	Hi.
MICHAEL	You guys are early.
ANDREW	No, seven, did you not…
MICHAEL	Oh I thought we said eight.
ANDREW	Oh seven, eight. Can't remember now really.
MICHAEL	I would have got back earlier.
RAFE	Honestly, it's fine.
PETE	I'm sure we said seven.
MICHAEL	I was gonna iron a shirt.

RAFE   Oh no… you don't have to do that…

MICHAEL   You two are always so smart though.

RAFE   Really?

MICHAEL   Yeah.

RAFE   I guess it's just a thing we've always done.

MICHAEL   No, I think it's great.
            Always very sharp.

RAFE   Well I'm glad we did; this is a really nice flat.

ANDREW   Oh. Well.

MICHAEL   If we didn't have the girls, it'd be perfect.

ANDREW   We'd like to get a place of our own.

PETE   Yeah Michael said.

ANDREW   [–]
            Did he?

PETE   Yeah.

MICHAEL   [–]
            …just a while back.

ANDREW   Right.

MICHAEL   We've been thinking about it for a while now
            really.

ANDREW   I mean it's such a step up.
            You know; rents at the moment.

RAFE   Sure.

PETE   Do you think you might buy at any point?

MICHAEL   No…

ANDREW   Buy?!
            Christ!
            Who can afford to buy?

RAFE   Yeah, no, exactly.

MICHAEL   We'll have to all move north in the end…
          Newcastle or…

PETE   Leeds.

MICHAEL   That's it.

RAFE   Urgh, my cousin lives in Leeds.
          His rent.
          You don't want to know…

MICHAEL   I could live in Leeds.

PETE   You don't want to live in Leeds.

RAFE   I could maybe live in Leeds.

PETE   You *don't* want to live in Leeds.

          [–]

ANDREW   Well look, I've buggered up so, let me get some
          drinks.
          Shall we stick with wine?

RAFE   Lovely.

PETE   / Wine'd be grand.

RAFE   Wine'd be lovely.

          ANDREW *exits*.

          [–]
          Where the *fuck* have you been?

MICHAEL   At the shops, where d'you think?

RAFE   You told him about us, didn't you?
          [–]
          He *knows* about us.

MICHAEL   No.

RAFE   Michael.

MICHAEL   Of course not…

PETE   (Rafe, it's fine, just leave it.)

MICHAEL   What's he said?

RAFE   Nothing is fine, Pete…
          Everything is wrong.

PETE   Rafe, will you chill out?

RAFE   Did you tell him, Michael?

MICHAEL   No.

RAFE   Promise?

MICHAEL   Yes.

RAFE   You'd better not have done.

MICHAEL   Or what?

PETE   *Rafe*.

RAFE   Have you?

MICHAEL   No…

RAFE   It's just.
          What was that campaign in the war?

MICHAEL   Campaign in the what?

RAFE   Those… poster things… on the Tube…

PETE   'Dig for victory'?

RAFE   No…

MICHAEL   'Don't fuck your friends'?

RAFE   [–]
          'Loose lips sink ships.'

          ANDREW *enters*.

ANDREW   [–]

          Sorry, did I [*interrupt something*]…?

RAFE   No, we were just, erm…

MICHAEL   [–]
          Gun crime.

RAFE   Yeah.

ANDREW   Gun crime?

MICHAEL   Uh-huh.

RAFE   It's really bad at the moment.

ANDREW   Is it?

PETE   (Mmm.)

ANDREW   Round here?

RAFE   Well...
            Everywhere.

PETE   [–]
            Thanks for this [*wine*].

RAFE   Yeah looks great.

ANDREW   Ah no it's just, cheap crap my mum picks up.
            (She does a booze cruise twice a year)
            (Tobacco mostly)
            (But anyway)
            You're welcome.
            And also: welcome.

PETE   Thanks Andrew.

ANDREW   Cheers.

RAFE   It's great to be here.

ANDREW   Yes.
            We'll have to have a glass of that prosecco in a bit.

PETE   Yeah sure.

ANDREW   Celebrate.

RAFE   Are we, celebrating?

ANDREW   No, not particularly.
            Just. Being alive I guess.
            Life.

MICHAEL   (to life…)

[–]

ANDREW   Oh I do have some news actually.

RAFE   [–]
Yeah?

PETE   [–]
What's that?

ANDREW   [–]
My sister's getting married.

RAFE   Aw.

PETE   That's great.

RAFE   Congratulations.

ANDREW   Thank you.

MICHAEL   Well…

RAFE   Oh… it's not good?

MICHAEL   It's not that it's not good, it's just…

ANDREW   It's sort of a bit soon.

RAFE   Oh, right.

ANDREW   She's only known him for six months.

RAFE   Yikes.

PETE   Whirlwind.

RAFE   How old is she?

ANDREW   Oh like, thirty-three?

PETE   There you go then.

MICHAEL   He proposed to her in *Paris*.

PETE   Really?

MICHAEL   *Such* a cliché.

RAFE   How is that a cliché?
            It's romantic.

MICHAEL   It's ridiculous.

PETE   Andrew, would you?

ANDREW   What?

PETE   Down on one knee…
            Beneath the Notre-Dame…

ANDREW   No, no…

MICHAEL   Anywhere *but*.
            Please.

RAFE   No, hang on.
            I feel the need to stick up for.
            What's his name?

ANDREW   Taylor.

RAFE   Taylor?

ANDREW   Yeah.

RAFE   That's actually his name?

PETE   What; is he foreign or something?
            Like, American…?

ANDREW   No, he's from Croydon.

RAFE   Right…
            Well, look.
            Okay?
            Imagine you're a guy, right?
            A straight guy, I mean.
            Is he… metrosexual, Taylor?

ANDREW   He works at Carphone Warehouse.

RAFE   Well there you go.
            Taylor comes from Croydon and he works at
            Carphone Warehouse.
            His general world view is potentially quite small.
            So he sees on TV…

                    (In a film or whatever…)
                    Sarah Jessica Parker.
                    Getting down on one knee.
                    (In front of the Eiffel Tower.)
                    For him it's not a *cliché*.
                    It's just what he's seen in films.

MICHAEL   Do straight guys watch films with Sarah Jessica
            Parker?

RAFE   (It's called *learned behaviour* actually; I watched
            a TED Talk about it.)

PETE   Yeah but if she's thirty-three…

RAFE   What?

PETE   She has to settle down.

RAFE   Why?

MICHAEL   Do I have to settle down?
            When I'm thirty-three?

PETE   Yeah but women have body clocks.
            We don't have to get married.
            I mean, our ovaries aren't going to rust.

MICHAEL   Nice.

RAFE   Nice image.

PETE   Well they're not.
            We can get married in our fifties if we want.

ANDREW   I hope not.

MICHAEL   (Why?)

RAFE   But if we wanted to adopt.
            (Which we do…)
            We'd still have to consider our age.
            Wouldn't we?

MICHAEL   What… if we wanna be heteros?

PETE   No, it's not about being *heteros*…

MICHAEL   Isn't it?

PETE   Course not.

MICHAEL   Thirty-three's… *kiddie time?*

PETE   Well for women it is.
It has to be.

MICHAEL   Hmm.

RAFE   Well look if she's ready to settle down, I don't see
the problem.
Perhaps she just knows.

ANDREW   We just think she's rushing a bit.
Panicking perhaps.

PETE   I'd panic if I were her.

RAFE   Well people just want to get on with their lives…
They want to take control.

ANDREW   [–]
I spoke to her yesterday actually.
My sister… Rosie.
(not about that, I'm sure her…
Ovaries are fine…
But…)
Something had happened at work.

MICHAEL   Really?

ANDREW   She was in a pretty bad way.

MICHAEL   You didn't say anything…

ANDREW   Well, the thing is.
What happened was…
She was showing her work mates photos of
their trip.
You know; croissants… berets…

PETE   Garlic.

ANDREW   Exactly.
And one of the women was like 'Ohhh, Taylor's
so good-looking…

Rosie, you're really lucky.'
And my sister sort of stopped.
And she was like… 'What do you mean?'
And the woman was like, 'Oh no, it's no big deal,
it's just. Taylor's really hot.'
And my sister was like 'Yeah…'
And the woman was like, well… she didn't carry
on or anything…
But she didn't really need to.
It was clear what she meant.

RAFE   *Is* Taylor hot?

MICHAEL   Very.

RAFE   And your sister?

PETE   (I don't follow…)

ANDREW   Well. I think what this woman was *trying* to say
was…
My sister's a different number.
Like, if Taylor's a ten then my sister's a sort of six.

PETE   Oh.

ANDREW   And it made her really upset.
Because…
Does that make them incompatible?

RAFE   No.

ANDREW   Should Taylor have found another nine or ten
instead?

RAFE   Of course not, no…

ANDREW   Should my sister have stuck to the sixes?
The kids who can't dance at the disco?
[–]
And I thought about it.
A lot.
About my sister and Taylor.
And the woman at work.
And then I thought about *me*.

[–]
About Michael.
[–]
Because Michael's a ten.
And I'm a sort of six.
(If we're being realistic.)
So what I want to know is.
(If you don't mind me asking.)
What I wanted to ask you was:
Why didn't you pick me?

[–]

Why did you pick Michael?

[–]

MICHAEL   Andrew. Come on.

PETE   What's all this picking thing?

RAFE   Did someone say something or?

ANDREW   ...to sleep with you.
[–]
I really won't mind.
[–]
I just... sort of need to know.

RAFE   [–]
Michael you swore on your mum's / life...

MICHAEL   No, I did not.
I specifically, did not.

ANDREW   Look, I'm not offended.
Honestly.
I'm just... curious... yeah.
Is it his body?
Or face or...
Did you think he'd be better in bed?

PETE   No, no...
Andrew, you're.
/ Way off the mark.

RAFE   Wrong end of the stick.

ANDREW   Was it tossing a coin or...
            Tossing off to our photos?

PETE   / Oh come on.

RAFE   Andrew that's disgusting.

ANDREW   Was this something you always thought about?
            Whenever we met up?
            Fantasised about across the snacks table at parties?

RAFE   No...
            No, of course not, no... it was just...

PETE   Rafe.

RAFE   What?

PETE   Look, come on, Andrew.
            I really don't think...

ANDREW   No go on Rafe.
            [–]
            What was it?

PETE   Look I think we should all just move on, okay?
            Admit it was a bad idea.

ANDREW   No.
            Come on.
            There was something.
            Wasn't there?
            What was it?

RAFE   [–]
            Michael was just.

PETE   Older.

ANDREW   Older...?

PETE   More experienced.

ANDREW   Right.
            A slag, you mean.

MICHAEL   Andrew.

ANDREW   What's the reason, Rafe?

MICHAEL   Come on now.

ANDREW   Cos Michael's more 'handsome'?

RAFE   No!

ANDREW   Michael goes to the *gym*?

PETE   It wasn't that at all.

ANDREW   So why did you pick him?

RAFE   Because…

PETE   Rafe.

ANDREW   What?

[–]

RAFE   Because Michael does this.

MICHAEL   …what?

RAFE   It's just… what we heard.

MICHAEL   Michael fucking 'does this'?

RAFE   And Andrew, you're so much more…
…*thoughtful* about things.
We knew you'd overthink it.

MICHAEL   Cos *I* don't think?

RAFE   Of course *not*…

MICHAEL   I'm not *thoughtful*?

PETE   That's not what we're saying…

RAFE   We thought Michael would go for this.
And it turned out he did.
He could have very easily said no.

PETE   It had nothing to do with the way you look.

ANDREW   I see.

RAFE   But telling you about it…
            That was *completely* off-limits.

ANDREW   Ah…

RAFE   Not on the agenda.

ANDREW   Well that's okay then.
            So long as *Andrew* doesn't find out… well…
            everything's okay!

RAFE   No… so that *this* right here, what's happening
            now…
            …would not happen.

ANDREW   Well that's kind of you; thank you.
            To protect my feelings.

RAFE   That's exactly how it was.

ANDREW   Cos my relationship's not as important as yours?

RAFE   No…

ANDREW   Cos we've not been together seven years?

MICHAEL   Look, Andrew and I have an open relationship.
            (Private, I might add but.)
            He knew about it from the start, okay…

RAFE   (A private open relationship?)

MICHAEL   So if you think you're like *revealing* something
            here?
            I told him from the off.

RAFE   Which we specifically said not to.
            In fact I particularly remember you swore on
            your mum's –

MICHAEL   I did not *swear* on my mother's life, Rafe.
            Over something so trivial.
            I'd swear on my mum's life if like
            Hitler were dangling my father off a cliff.
            But you're asking about a shag here.
            And to be honest with you Rafe.
            The whole situation's been nothing but a pain.

I mean no wonder you guys are in a crisis here.
You're so desperately hanging on.
[–]
Of course I was going to tell him.

RAFE   Sorry; 'desperately hanging on'?

MICHAEL   Well aren't you?

            [–]

ANDREW   Michael does this with *who*?

PETE   [–]
            What?

ANDREW   Michael does this with who?
            [–]
            Because Michael and I have an arrangement.
            And yes it might be *unusual* to you.
            But the arrangement is that it's with someone
            neither of us knows.
            – a stranger.
            – an encounter.
            – Grindr; that's fine.
            – if we're away on business, whatever…
            But it can
            – never be a friend.
            – never be someone we both know.
            – and never more than once.
            They're the rules.
            But seeing as though we know both of you the
            same;
            Who would these people be?
            These people to whom it's known?

RAFE   Just like…
            People.

            [–]
            [–]
            [–]

            Andy Fountain.

ANDREW   [–]
          Andy Fountain?

MICHAEL   It was like… one time.

ANDREW   Who else?

PETE   That's it.
          [–]
          That's all that we know.

ANDREW   No come on, who do you know?

PETE   No one.

ANDREW   Yes you do.
          People is plural.
          Who do you know, Pete?

PETE   Nobody.

          [–]

RAFE   Sam Evans.

PETE   *Rafe*.

RAFE   What? He wants to know.

ANDREW   Sam fucking Evans?

MICHAEL   Ages ago…
          I'd been seeing him before and.

ANDREW   And they chat about it, do they?
          These people?

PETE   No.

ANDREW   On WhatsApp?

PETE   No.

ANDREW   'Idle gossip.'

PETE   Of course they don't.

RAFE   Oh come on.

PETE   Leave it, Rafe.

RAFE   No!
            He has a reputation.

MICHAEL   I beg your pardon…?

RAFE   We even saw a picture of his cock once.

MICHAEL   Bullshit.

PETE   *Rafe.*

MICHAEL   Rafe, fuck you.

RAFE   Well why should we lie?
            It isn't fair on Andrew.

PETE   (What the fuck are you doing?)

RAFE   Well if *we* know about it, why shouldn't he?
            Everyone else does.

PETE   No they don't.

ANDREW   Do they?

RAFE   Course they do.

PETE   (That's overstepping a mark.)

RAFE   (No, it's not fair.)

ANDREW   I appreciate that, Rafe.

MICHAEL   No one saw a picture of my dick.
            You were probably looking in the mirror for
            Christ's sake.

ANDREW   Who else?
            Anyone?

PETE   There's nobody else.

ANDREW   Is there, Rafe?
            [–]
            Rafe?

RAFE   [–]
            There's no one else.

            [–]

ANDREW   Well.
          I think this is the part where we clink our glasses
          and talk about holidays.
          (They're saying Latvia's on the rise but…)
          [–]
          …actually I think the two of you should just [*go*]…

RAFE   This really, Andrew, seriously. Like.

          [–]

          This was never supposed to be like this.
          Honestly.
          We promise.

ANDREW   Right.

RAFE   [–]
          I hope we can still be friends.

ANDREW   Is that what we are? Friends?

RAFE   Of course we are…
          Meet up…?
          …have a drink?

ANDREW   (Rubbish.)

PETE   What?

ANDREW   (It's bollocks.)
          We haven't been friends for years…

RAFE   Haven't we?

ANDREW   Ever since Pete started earning money.
          Like that makes you some sort of…
          Transformative.
          Superior.
          I mean.
          The clothes and.

PETE   Our clothes?

ANDREW   *Prosecco.*
          What's that?
          You used to bring beers.

PETE   We drink prosecco...
            So what?

ANDREW   With a nice little side of sundried tomatoes.
            Sorry, *sunblushed*.

PETE   I don't know where this has come from Andrew
            but...

ANDREW   You know, I loved you guys at uni because you
            were young and passionate and we talked about
            what we'd do with our lives and how we'd make
            the world a better place.
            Well I stuck to that.
            Didn't I?
            You on the other hand...

PETE   (Is this what you think?)

ANDREW   With your bottles of prosecco.
            And... Ralph Lauren shirts.
            Like... 'Bring on the sloe gin.'

PETE   What do you want me to do, apologise?

ANDREW   But it's not real; is it?
            Any of it...
            – *Simply Nigella*.
            – Pot plants.
            – Trips to the zoo.
            It's all just for show.

PETE   You do it too.

ANDREW   Of course.
            Everyone does.
            But what about *happiness*?
            (off-camera that is)
            What exactly's that?
            Fucking each other's boyfriends?

RAFE   Let's just go.

ANDREW   Put *that* on Instagram perhaps...
            (See if it gets some 'likes'.)

PETE   Maybe we will.

ANDREW   What you have to think about Pete is what you
            actually want to achieve.
            When you're eighty years old and look back at
            what you've done…
            What exactly will that be?
            A husband, family?
            Bits on the side?
            Going behind Rafe's back perhaps…

PETE   I think this is exactly why we don't hang out with
            you any more Andrew…

ANDREW   But then again what exactly do you expect from
            someone like you.

PETE   What does that even mean?

ANDREW   Well, come on, let's face it: no one stands up in
            their childhood assembly and says 'When I grow
            up I'd like to work for KPMG.'
            And yet somehow people do.
            Cos they wake up one morning and they realise
            they're cunts.
            And where do cunts go?
            KPMG.

            [–]

RAFE   Look I'm sorry we chose Michael, Andrew.
            I'm sorry we didn't pick you.
            There's no need to get personal.

ANDREW   Yeah well there was no need to come in here and
            fuck my boyfriend but that didn't stop you either
            did it.
            But let's not 'get personal'.
            [–]

RAFE   We really are sorry.
            And we're sorry about the [*threesome*] thing?
            Before?

ANDREW   You think I actually wanted a threesome?

PETE   [–]
            I think you did.

            [–]

            RAFE *and* PETE *exit*.

            [–]

MICHAEL   Andrew.

ANDREW   [–]

            [–]
            [–]
            [–]

            I remember when we first hooked up.
            I thought fuck I've done well.

MICHAEL   Don't be ridiculous.

ANDREW   I'm not.
            For the first year of our relationship I was
            convinced I'd wake up and you'd have buggered
            off elsewhere.
            You even get come on to in the checkout queue
            at Asda.

MICHAEL   No I don't.

ANDREW   Yes you do.
            It's the reason you live in the gym.
            Loving the attention…

MICHAEL   Look, *you* are my boyfriend.
            For a very good reason.

ANDREW   And what would that reason be?

MICHAEL   I love you.

ANDREW   Oh come on.
            That's what fourteen-year-old boys say when
            they want to finger a girl round the back of the
            bike sheds.

MICHAEL   I *only* love you.

ANDREW   But you also love fucking around.
          If we're being honest.

MICHAEL   [–]

ANDREW   Andy Fountain
          Sam Evans.

MICHAEL   I don't give a shit about them.

ANDREW   They've seen a picture of your *cock*.

MICHAEL   It must be from Grindr.

ANDREW   Oh well…
          Brilliant!
          It's probably just from Grindr…
          That makes me feel a whole lot better.
          [–]
          You've made me look like a total fucking twat.
          What did I do to you?
          Come on.
          What did I do to you?
          Nothing… at *all*.
          I have been a good fucking boyfriend.
          I've stood by you and stayed with you and…
          Why would you sleep with Andy Fountain?
          He is such a cliché.
          How many times?

MICHAEL   Andrew…

ANDREW   How many times?

MICHAEL   I don't know…
          A couple…

ANDREW   A couple… right…
          So it's actually more like five or ten or?

MICHAEL   Look, we sleep together, don't we?
          Eat together, right?
          Shower together, Andrew.
          I even piss in front of you.

ANDREW   Which you know I can't stand.

MICHAEL   I *would* have buggered off if this wasn't what I
           wanted.
           But it *is*.

ANDREW   Is it?

MICHAEL   Of course.

ANDREW   So Andy Fountain's... what?

MICHAEL   Stupid.
           Meaningless. Thick as shit. You know that.

ANDREW   And yet still I'm not enough, am I?
           Still I'm not some... Aryan god like him?
           Cos I don't have a *physique* like his...

MICHAEL   No...

ANDREW   Michael has biceps.
           Michael's got obliques.
           Andrew's just a bit funny looking.

MICHAEL   Andrew you're gorgeous.

ANDREW   And yet actually Michael, you've never managed
           to tell me that.

MICHAEL   Of course I have.

ANDREW   Never.
           Not once.
           In three whole years.
           [–]
           Why do you fuck other guys?

MICHAEL   For the same reason as you.
           Variety.

ANDREW   Ohhh...

MICHAEL   It stops us getting bored.

ANDREW   Because I'm boring?

MICHAEL   No...

ANDREW   Because I don't have obliques...

MICHAEL   You do it too.

ANDREW   Right…

MICHAEL   Don't put this all on me.

ANDREW   Because you're the one who asks for it.
            You're the one who wants it.

MICHAEL   You don't have to do it.
            [–]
            Why do you?

ANDREW   [–]
            For a little bit of *pride* perhaps?
            So I'm not consistently off-balance?

MICHAEL   I should never have done it…
            Rafe and Pete.
            I went too far…

ANDREW   At least I *knew* about them.
            Andy Fountain?
            Sam Evans?
            How the fuck can I forgive you?
            [–]

MICHAEL   You know how I feel.
            Monogamy scares me.

ANDREW   [–]
            Spiders are scary.
            [–]
            Terrorists are scary.
            Cancer is *really* scary.
            Monogamy?

MICHAEL   [–]
            Well what do you want to do then?
            Do you want us to break up?
            Do you want us to take a break, or?

ANDREW   [–]

MICHAEL   I don't want that, do you?
            [–]

But ask yourself this…
Do you really want to have sex with the same
person week after week for the rest of your life?
Become this, second-rate version of the people we
used to be?
– Not talking in restaurants…
– Making weather observations.
– Reading a bloody *Kindle* in bed?
Where's the excitement in that?
You're telling me you won't get *bored*?
[–]
Or else we have a little bit of leeway.
A little bit of a room to go 'yeah you know what';
these things happen but that's okay because I'm
comfortable with this.
I am comfortable with him.
[–]

ANDREW   What and that's it?
           'The best of both worlds'?

MICHAEL   No…

ANDREW   Sounds that way.
           [–]
           Sounds greedy to me.

MICHAEL   It's not greedy Andrew…
           It's just…
           If that's what works.

ANDREW   [–]
           Well then maybe you could tell that to the rest of
           the world.
           Get it written in to the wedding vows perhaps.
           'To have and to hold'
           …'And a few others too…'
           Cos that's what we do…
           [–]
           That's just what *we* do.
           [–]

I don't think those are the vows I want to write…
[–]
We didn't come this far to throw everything away
on a meaningless shag when you're a little bit
drunk round the back of a Tesco.
And if that's *my* problem for *me* to work out then
I'm sure you'll find a person who happily goes
along with the life you want.
And for your sake, Michael, I really hope you do.
[–]

I'm gonna go stay with Rosie for a bit.

MICHAEL   Andrew.
Please…

ANDREW   This has been.
[–]
Amazing.
But.
[–]
I have to take control of this.

MICHAEL   [–]
Is that really the answer…?

ANDREW   I think it is, yeah.

MICHAEL   [–]
That's really what you want?

ANDREW   [–]
What I want is for you to sleep next to me in bed
at night and for that to be enough.
For me to be your… absolute everything.
[–]
I don't think that's a lot to ask.

MICHAEL   I want that too.

ANDREW   Do you?

MICHAEL   Yes.

ANDREW   *Do you?*

MICHAEL   [–]
           Yes.

ANDREW   Then get there, Michael.
           Get there.
           [–]
           Because otherwise, yeah…
           [–]
           I will leave, yeah.

MICHAEL   Please don't.

ANDREW   Then give me a reason to stay.
           [–]
           Michael?
           [–]
           Give me a reason to stay.

Twelve

RAFE *watches Netflix.*

Thirteen

PETE *and* MICHAEL.

       [–]

MICHAEL   You've done this before.
              [–]
              Haven't you?

PETE   Done what?

MICHAEL   *This*.
              With other guys.

PETE   No.

MICHAEL   *Sure*.

PETE   Of course I haven't.

MICHAEL   Right.

PETE   Michael…
              [–]
              I haven't.

MICHAEL   Okay, fine…

PETE   No…
              Don't 'fine' me.
              You're the only one, okay?
              So I don't know if you want to feel like.
              Privileged or whatever.
              If it earns you, what…
              Brownie points…

MICHAEL   I mean, it was you who suggested it.
              Wasn't it?
              That does suggest to me that this is what you do.

PETE   You're not allowed it either.
              It goes against your rules.
              a) you know me, b) it's more than once.
              and c) after everything that's happened?

MICHAEL   Maybe we'll stop then.

PETE   What, miss out on this?
            Yeah right.

MICHAEL   Don't flatter yourself.

PETE   I'm not.

MICHAEL   You want this more than I do.

PETE   [–]
            You and Andy Fountain were fucking for months.

MICHAEL   [–]
            And...?

PETE   He told us he'd fallen in love with you.
            [–]
            Does Andrew know about that?

MICHAEL   Does Rafe know about this?
            [–]
            We can't keep doing it, you know.

PETE   Why not?

MICHAEL   It's not a good idea.

PETE   It doesn't hurt anyone, does it?

MICHAEL   If a tree falls in the woods, you mean.

PETE   Something like that.

MICHAEL   You couldn't live with yourself.

PETE   Why not?

MICHAEL   Cos I know what you're like.

PETE   No you don't.

MICHAEL   Things like this always come out.
            You promise they won't but they always do.

PETE   It can't.

MICHAEL   Yeah; that's what they always say.

PETE   It won't let it happen.
            There's too much at stake.

MICHAEL   They say that too.
           It's very routine.

PETE   It's not going to come out.

MICHAEL   Sure.

PETE   Michael:
           It won't come out.

MICHAEL   Fine.

           [–]

PETE   Do you want to get some dinner?

MICHAEL   No I've got to go.

PETE   Home or...

MICHAEL   Yep.

PETE   [–]
           You know Rafe's away till Sunday.
           If you wanted to maybe stay one night...

MICHAEL   Is this what you think this is?

PETE   [–]
           Just saying.

MICHAEL   [–]
           I'll see you around some time.

PETE   What, is that it?

MICHAEL   [–]

PETE   Don't I get a kiss?

MICHAEL   [–]

           Look, Pete...

PETE   *Okay...*

MICHAEL   That's not what this is, alright..

PETE   Look I wasn't asking for a thesis or anything.
           Jesus...

MICHAEL   You've got the wrong idea.

PETE   Forget it, alright.
Christ.

MICHAEL   [–]

PETE   I said alright.

MICHAEL   [–]
Do you mind if I tell you something personal?

PETE   So long as you don't have like, gonorrhoea or
something.

MICHAEL   It's about my mum and dad.

PETE   Alright.

MICHAEL   When I was fifteen years old the two of them got
divorced.
It was an amicable split.
They just fell out of love.

PETE   Sorry what's this got to do with…

MICHAEL   Just hear me out, okay?
[–]
What it came to down to was:
They were looking for different things.
The next part of their life.
Someone else to be *happier* with.
They didn't get to the stage of hurting each other
and, messing each other around. They tried to
make it work, but they couldn't so they split.
They both walked away with their dignity intact.

PETE   Are you really trying to give *me* a lecture about
morals?

MICHAEL   The question you have to ask yourself is:
Would you rather jump ship?
(when the waters get a bit choppy?)
Or do you try and sail back to shore?

PETE   Oh I'm a vessel now am I?

MICHAEL   You both want different things.
            Rafe wants to get back to land.
            To get back to what you had but.
            You'd stay out at sea.
            Drinking all night on the party boat.
            Sailing out to islands / and.

PETE   Will you stop with the fucking metaphors about
            your parents and... seamen?
            [–]

MICHAEL   And this...
            Already.
            Seeing you again.
            It becomes about something else.
            It becomes about something more.

PETE   I know you like me, Michael.

MICHAEL   I like a lot of people.
            So what?

PETE   Not but *really* like me.
            And I like you.
            As in *really* like you.

MICHAEL   No you don't.
            What you like is the *idea* of me.
            Fucking all these people.
            You think Andrew and I have something
            aspirational.
            But honestly, you shouldn't.
            (You really shouldn't...)

PETE   Why not?

MICHAEL   Because I'm a terrible person;
            – I cheat on Andrew.
            – I fuck other guys.
            – I have absolutely *no restraint*.
            You think that's nice?

PETE   If that's what works...

MICHAEL   I come in drunk in the middle of the night and
            Andrew's in bed watching YouTube in his onesie.
            He can't get to sleep till he knows I'm home.
            And some nights I don't come home.
            That doesn't *work*, does it?
            [–]
            You think you and I would have some... what?
            Walk into the sunset?
            Bullshit.
            I'd do exactly what I do to Andrew.
            And there's two things that'd happen:
            Either you'd accept it and it'd just be this
            unspoken thing between us or you wouldn't know
            it was happening in the first place and then you'd
            look like such a fucking idiot.

PETE   Like Andrew?

MICHAEL   Like Rafe?

PETE   So why does he stay with you?

MICHAEL   [–]
            Look, I should have told you before but...
            Rafe and I didn't actually sleep together.
            We didn't even kiss.
            We just talked.

PETE   [–]
            Why?

MICHAEL   He said his head was a mess and that it wasn't
            his idea.

PETE   It was mine.
            You know that.

MICHAEL   He told me you wanted to do this in order to 'save
            your relationship'?

PETE   I thought it might help.

MICHAEL   How?

PETE   To find an arrangement.

MICHAEL   Like mine?

PETE   Perhaps.

MICHAEL   It doesn't work like that.
            You can't just transition to something like this.

PETE   I hoped we could.

MICHAEL   Well you can't.

PETE   It didn't stop you though, did it?

MICHAEL   What didn't?

PETE   Rafe.
            You still did it anyway.
            (With me that is.)
            That says something, doesn't it?

MICHAEL   I did it because Rafe *begged* me to.
            He said if you didn't sleep with someone else
            you'd leave him.
            He did this to save your relationship.
            And now look…!

PETE   But what about us?
            Hmm?
            If I broke up with Rafe?
            Could we have something like this?

MICHAEL   Us?

PETE   Yes, us.

MICHAEL   Pete, come on.
            Are you actually saying this?

PETE   Don't you think about it?

MICHAEL   No.

PETE   What the two of us would be like?

MICHAEL   [–]
          D'you wanna know what I think about, Pete?
          About men?
          …about guys?
          [–]
          I think all of us.
          Every guy.
          Before we leave the house.
          We should all just…
          Wank.
          Think of all the problems it would solve.
          You'd sit in your bedroom
          (bathroom, whatever)
          And
          Wank it all out.
          All these. Repressed emotions and.
          Difficulties.
          Infidelities.
          The answer to cheating lies in a very small amount
          of liquid you eject from your body.
          The key to so many problems.
          Cos if you don't have a wank.
          It only ever leads to more.
          You just follow things through.
          It's instinctive, of course.
          Animalistic, you might say.
          But as soon as it comes.
          (Literally. Cums.)
          In that moment afterwards.
          You don't feel good.
          You don't feel hot.
          You feel fucking terrible.
          Dirty.
          Bad.
          What a waste of time that was.
          All the pursuing.
          The chasing.
          For what?
          What for?

[–]
I love my boyfriend, Pete.
All this has to stop.
All this makes me feel is dirty and horrible and.
I am *in* love with Andrew.
You might think I'm some kind of, poster boy…
But I'm not.
I feel like I'm…
(I dunno…)
Anorexic or something.
Like it's become a problem just to eat.
And all I want to do is enjoy the food I've got.
So this.
All this?
It all has to stop…
I have to go exclusive.

PETE   It's easy for you to say that.
            [–]
            When it's on the other foot…

MICHAEL   But I have to give it a go.
            I can't keep doing this…
            I've fucked up way too much.

PETE   Michael, come on…
            I need this.

MICHAEL   No…

PETE   Do it for me…

MICHAEL   No, I'm done with it…

PETE   Please?

MICHAEL   Look, I'm gonna go now.

PETE   No…
            Come on…
            I know that you like me.

MICHAEL   Sort yourself out, Pete.

PETE   We have something here.

MICHAEL   Right.

PETE   I *know* you want it too…

MICHAEL   If that's what you want to believe.

PETE   You *like me*.
            I know you do.

MICHAEL   God listen to yourself, Pete!
            Begging!
            For fuck's sake.
            [–]
            You're embarrassing yourself.

PETE   [–]
            I'll tell Andrew.
            About this.

MICHAEL   Tell him.
            Go on.
            Ring him up right now.
            You'd be doing me a favour.
            Maybe I'll call Rafe.

PETE   You wouldn't dare.

MICHAEL   Wouldn't I?
            It'd do you the world of good.

PETE   [–]
            And we really can't ever just… casually perhaps?

MICHAEL   No.

PETE   Just for a bit of fun or…?

MICHAEL   Never again.

PETE   Why not?

MICHAEL   Because it's not a good idea.

PETE   Why not?

MICHAEL   Because it's not a good idea.

PETE   Why not?

           [–]

MICHAEL   Because it's not a good idea.

Fourteen

RAFE *and* PETE.

           [–]

PETE   What is this just… how it's going to be now?

RAFE   Maybe.

PETE   That's mature.

RAFE   I don't particularly feel like I have anything to say
           to you.

PETE   So what you'll just ignore me?

RAFE   Probably.

PETE   Great.
           [–]
           Well I guess I'll look forward to that.
           Bit of quiet for a change.

           [–]

           God, say something Rafe.

RAFE   What do you want me to say?
           What do you want me to *say*?

PETE   Look what was supposed to happen?
           Huh?
           Was this supposed to just go on?
           …indefinitely into the future?

RAFE   *I* thought so.

PETE   Yeah and I did too.

RAFE   Right.

PETE   One day.
Course I did.
If no one believed in anything then no one'd ever
go anywhere, would they?
But I tried.
Okay?
At *least* give me that.

RAFE   We have two copies of REM's *Greatest Hits*.
One of them is missing its CD.
Do you want it?

PETE   Rafe.

RAFE   These things have to be decided, Pete.

PETE   You really can't see…?
Seven years?
You can't see how that's unhealthy?

RAFE   Seven-and-a-half.
[–]
Not that you ever really remember stuff like that.

PETE   Yes I do.

RAFE   You barely remember my birthday.

PETE   March 21st.

RAFE   I'll text you my address then.
Perhaps you can send me a card.
[–]
I'm staying at my mum's for a bit.
Not that you care.
You never really liked her very much.

PETE   [–]
Look… Rafe…

RAFE   (Nice bit of denial there…)

PETE   Look at my face in this – [*a photo*].
        Look at that smile.
        What… do you think that was just *Splash
        Mountain?*
        No…
        It was you. And me…
        Being together.
        I loved you so hard.
        [–]
        So if there's any consolation to take from this,
        Rafe.
        At least we *tried*.

RAFE   That's not a consolation.

PETE   We didn't walk away.

RAFE   A consolation'd be like, oh yeah he died but…
        secretly he was a millionaire… Or…
        Ahh second place but here's a giant fucking
        teddy bear…
        What's the consolation here?

PETE   That it was the right thing to *try*…

RAFE   To save our relationship?

PETE   Yes. Don't you think?

RAFE   I don't think so, no.

PETE   But better that we tried than just, straight-up
        jump ship?

RAFE   I don't really need CDs any more; I've got Spotify
        instead.
        You can take it.
        Really.

PETE   Why are you making me the bad guy in this?
        Give me some credit, okay?
        Credit where it's due.
        I tried. Did I not?

Come on. I tried.
What did you do? Hmm?
What did you *ever* do?
You just bobbed along.
Gently.
Never asked questions.
Turned your back.
Why can't you just face up to these things, Rafe?
[–]
Face your fucking problems.

RAFE   We said we wouldn't do this.

PETE   Then don't blame me, okay?
Do not do that.
Cos you spawned this shit just as much as I did
and I am not going to sit back and be the bad guy
in this...
I will not be that person...
[–]
And I'll tell you something else, when I walk out
of that door it will not be to silence...
I will find myself someone who talks about these
things.

RAFE   Good luck with that, yeah?

PETE   I don't need luck, Rafe, I do not need *luck*.

RAFE   [–]
In those seven-and-a-half years.
I want you to tell me.
Were you faithful to me?
[–]
Pete. Look me in the eyes and tell me you were
faithful.

PETE   [–]
Do you know what, Rafe?
I really hate REM.
I really fucking hate them.
[–]

Fifteen

ANDREW *and* RAFE.

       [–]

ANDREW   Rafe.
                  Hey.

RAFE   Oh, hi.

ANDREW   You here by yourself…?

RAFE   [–]
                  Yeah, yeah…

ANDREW   You wanna join?

RAFE   Oh no…
                  Honestly.

ANDREW   You sure?

RAFE   No, really… I…
                  Like coming by myself.
                  No one else to.
                  Distract or.
                  Give their opinion.

ANDREW   Sure.

RAFE   How are…
                  How are you…
                  Are you well, are you…

ANDREW   Yeah.

RAFE   You're looking really well.

ANDREW   Thank you.
                  You too.

RAFE   Yeah, I'm.
                  (thanks)
                  [–]
                  Yeah I'm okay.

ANDREW   [–]
                   Not seen you in ages.

RAFE   No.

ANDREW   How are things?

RAFE   Yeah not too bad actually...
                   [–]
                   I'm in this house-share now.
                   I found a place on Gumtree.
                   (Really nice place actually.)
                   (Just round the corner)

ANDREW   Sounds good.

RAFE   Yeah.
                   Two girls and me so.
                   We have some fun.

ANDREW   Sounds nice.

RAFE   Yeah it's.
                   [–]
                   Yeah.

ANDREW   Good.
                   [–]
                   Great.

RAFE   And you...
                   Things are.

ANDREW   Yeah.

RAFE   Right.
                   Good.
                   Good.
                   That's. Great.

                   [–]

                   You know, Andrew.

ANDREW   No, Rafe...
                   Honestly.

RAFE   No, I just have to say…

ANDREW   Honestly, Rafe.
            [–]
            Really.

RAFE   [–]
            Sorry, I.
            [–]
            Right.

            [–]

            MICHAEL *enters*.

MICHAEL   Hello, stranger…

RAFE   Oh, hey…
            Michael…

MICHAEL   Nice to see you.
            How are you?

RAFE   Yeah, yeah, erm, fine, yes, thanks.

MICHAEL   Hey congratulations.

RAFE   Erm…?

MICHAEL   You got a new job, right?

RAFE   Oh!
            …yeah.

MICHAEL   A promotion?

RAFE   That's right…
            (Sorry; totally forgot.)

MICHAEL   Exciting times.

RAFE   I…

MICHAEL   You must be really pleased.

RAFE   Yeah, course…
            It's…
            Keeping me busy.
            [–]

MICHAEL   I'm.
           We're sorry to hear about you and Pete.

RAFE   Thank you.

MICHAEL   Everything… okay?

RAFE   Oh yeah… Yes.
           I mean I guess it was sort of mutual really.
           Both of us knew it was going that way so.
           I think it's for the best.

MICHAEL   Course.

RAFE   We're. Young.
           And.
           [–]
           I'm looking forward to a bit of.
           Me time, I guess.
           [–]
           …time by myself.
           I mean seven years is a long time.

MICHAEL   Seven-and-a-half.

RAFE   Yeah.
           [–]
           A very long time.
           [–]
           Anyway…
           I've… heard he's having fun.

           [–]

           He seems very happy.

MICHAEL   Right, well.

RAFE   …yeah.

           [–]

           I'd better go in.

ANDREW   Sure.

RAFE   (I kinda like the trailers…)

MICHAEL   Course.
            Enjoy.

RAFE   Thank you; you too.

ANDREW   Are you sure you don't wanna...

RAFE   No, no...
            Honestly, thanks.
            It was good to see you, though.
            Take care.

            RAFE *exits*.

ANDREW   You too.

            [–]
            [–]

MICHAEL   Do you have the, erm...
            Tickets?

ANDREW   Yeah.
            Do you want anything else?
            Sweets...
            Popcorn?

MICHAEL   No I'm fine.
            Shall we go in?

ANDREW   [–]
            You know.
            Michael.
            When we were.
            Before.
            When the two of us were...
            'Open'?
            [–]
            I never slept with anyone else.
            [–]
            Just so you know.
            [–]
            And I'm not asking for like a.

Biography or.
List.
But I just want you to know that.
That that's what I did.
Or.
Didn't do.
Just so you know.

MICHAEL   Thank you.

ANDREW   Do you think we should buy some sweets?
[–]
Some food or.
No.
[–]
We're both okay without.
[–]
We'll be alright without.
[–]
What is it then, screen nine?

End.

A Nick Hern Book

Four Play first published in Great Britain in 2016 as a paperback original by Nick Hern Books Limited, The Glasshouse, 49a Goldhawk Road, London W12 8QP, in association with Fools and Kings, DEM Productions, and Theatre503, London

Four Play copyright © 2016 Jake Brunger

Jake Brunger has asserted his moral right to be identified as the author of this work

Cover photograph by Jack Sain

Designed and typeset by Nick Hern Books, London
Printed in the UK by Mimeo Ltd, Huntingdon, Cambridgeshire PE29 6XX

A CIP catalogue record for this book is available from the British Library

ISBN   978 1 84842 555 2

www.nickhernbooks.co.uk

facebook.com/nickhernbooks

twitter.com/nickhernbooks